Dedication

This book is dedicated to my beloved pastors and faithful staff at Calvary Chapel South Bay. Your passion for Christ and unfailing loyalty have helped me preach without apology or embarrassment. To each of you who have poured out your life for others and have labored in furthering the Gospel, I dedicate this book.

CROSSING THE LINE

THE COMPROMISED LIFE

Steve Mays

Published by Word for Life, Gardena, CA

ISBN 978-0-9826042-1-2

Printed in the United States of America

TABLE OF
CONTENTS

Solomon, the wisest of all mankind, wrote *"of the making of many books there is no end."* With today's exploding technology, advancing knowledge, and the ability to retrieve limitless books and publications, is it possible that King Solomon was also plagued by other writers who were no match for his wisdom and insights? Were they vying for his attention and endorsement? Most readers seem to prefer holding a hard copy, and so, reading shows little decline. Why another book?

Steve Mays demonstrates his resolve and commitment to living the life of Christ with dedication and to leading others in discovering God's purpose for their lives. When you read between the lines, you see that life's choices always have consequences. What appears to be attractive and pleasing can be an illusion. Perceptions are never reality but are often a cloudy distortion of consequences. Steve has lived a life of reality, and his life principles and stories give insight to help the reader reflect for his or her own personal application.

Steve has academic credentials equal to authors in the most popular markets today. His uniqueness comes from his unusual life and personal experiences from the gutter of brokenness and addiction and from his being utterly lost before he experienced the grace of God. Today he is a spiritual leader, an effective preacher and teacher of the Word of God, a builder of church and educational facilities, and an example of a transformed life. His ministry and service to the community are a witness of sacrificial work for the transformation of others.

"Many are called, but few are chosen," Jesus said, teaching of the two roads in life—the broad and the narrow. The offramps a person chooses ignore the truth of abundant life by rejection or neglect. Steve Mays' life journey shows no detours or contradictions of his choice of the narrow road, which always leads to life eternal. His writings and his teaching form a long line of God's power in the work of redemption and reconciliation. Any promise that offers the divine purpose for a transcendent, fulfilling life should lead to asking, "How does that apply to me?" This is not a question of self-centeredness, but a quest to fill the emptiness of life without God. For the follower of Christ, it requires the highest commitment to and the receiving of, by faith in the Lord Jesus as personal Savior and Lord, God's power in the Spirit-filled life.

Steve is respectfully and lovingly called "Pastor Steve." This simple title translates from more than 30 years as the pastor and faithful shepherd of Calvary Chapel South Bay in the center of urban Los Angeles. His congregation is composed of more than 20 different ethnic and cultural communities. His goal has always been to preach Christ and not culture, to unite and not to differentiate. He has repeatedly been honored by the mayors, law enforcement officials, and civic leadership of the cities surrounding the church. Even so, a spiritual leader has no more important legacy than his personal integrity. He has exemplified this in an unswerving commitment to the gospel of the Lord Jesus Christ and in his service in the steps of the Savior. In this, his latest book, he helps the reader to not "cross the line" of disobedience but to walk in obedience to the Lord.

> *"The Spirit of the Lord God is upon Me, because the LORD has anointed Me to preach good tidings to the poor. He has sent Me to heal the brokenhearted, to proclaim liberty to the captives, and the opening of the prison to those who are bound." Isaiah 61:1*

Ross Rhoads
Chaplain, Billy Graham Association

Samson's life in the book of Judges is an extraordinary story that offers many rich lessons for our lives. His story includes a miraculous birth, a godly heritage, and a special call. However, it's also a story about rebellion, lust, and selfishness. It reads like a great, timeless, best-selling novel. It is about a man chosen by God who has special gifts and supernatural abilities but who is also plagued with enemies in every corner—both internal enemies, like lust and selfishness, as well as external ones, like deceit and scandalous relationships. Like all great stories, there is also a hero in Samson, whose road to redemption is no less dramatic than his beginning. Surrounded by personal failure and locked away in the enemy's prison, Samson is humbled, forgiven, restored, and redeemed. The only difference between Samson's story and one on a trendy best-seller list is that Samson's story is all true. Most importantly, the same God who redeemed Samson is the same God on His throne today.

Samson is an example of how a life of spiritual compromise can debilitate a person. Even though Samson was gifted with Superman-like strength, his constant yielding to sin left him spiritually weak. But when Samson finally trusted in the Lord, then he was right where God needed him to be. He is ready to be reused by God Himself to fulfill all the purposes that God had appointed for him from the beginning of time. Samson becomes our hero once and for all. His faith and God's grace are his entrance into the *Hall of Faith* in the book of Hebrews, chapter 11.

Now, here's the encouragement for us: In spite of us being just like Samson in so many ways, amazingly, God has our place reserved in the Hall of Faith in spite of our shortcomings. *"How can that be?"* we wonder. *"I do not have supernatural strength, nor did an angel prophesy my birth."* Maybe not, but we are all gifted and chosen by God to fulfill His plans for us on this earth. Every day, each of us has the challenge either to yield to our flesh or to yield to the Spirit of God. We are not much different than our hero Samson. We all are attracted to the world; we all lust; and every wrong choice we make puts a little roadblock between us and our fellowship with God.

Let's learn from Samson. We don't have to live a life of habitual sin, yielding to every temptation that Satan sets before us. We don't have to cross that line. The Holy Spirit lives in us. We have God's presence in our lives and in our hearts. We have God's Word and the fellowship of His saints. It is my prayer that the Holy Spirit will speak to each of us as we journey together through Samson's life—an amazing story of a hero's divine call, worldly rebellion, and ultimate redemption.

Chapter 1

ARE YOU WASTING YOUR LIFE?

"And all these, having obtained a good testimony through faith . . ."
(Hebrews 11:39)

Many words could be used to describe Samson. He was supernaturally strong. He was a judge for the children of Israel, and he was a Nazirite. Samson was born for greatness. He was destined to destroy the Philistines and to set the Israelites free from destructive influences. However, Samson was also, undeniably, a man who struggled with lust. There isn't any other way to put it—he was a fleshly man. Selfishness ruled his life. Lust repeatedly destroyed and wasted his life despite the many opportunities God gave him to repent and do what he was born to do. Yet through God's grace, during the last few minutes of his life, Samson was given a final opportunity by the Lord to do what was right. Fortunately for Israel, Samson took it.

There are many lessons we can learn about selfishness, rebellion, and grace from the life of Samson. He was a man who continually pursued his own passions and desires instead of God's Word and will. He repeatedly disobeyed

God by choosing to serve himself rather than the Lord. He played too close to the edge and relied solely on himself as his own rescuer, never acknowledging God as the source of his gifting and strength. Samson perceived every act of mercy in his life as freedom to sin even more. Toward the end of his life, he didn't even realize that the Spirit of God had departed from him. What a sobering thought that God would remove His hand of favor from our lives and leave us to our own will. But God's grace prevailed in Samson's life, as it does in ours.

Samson made many mistakes, choosing to do most things the wrong way. One of the saddest realizations about Samson is that he didn't see God in his life until the very end. Yet it was God who intervened in his life at every turn. God sent a lion to protect Samson from going into a vineyard; He also sent His Spirit to give Samson the strength to overcome the lion (Judges 14:5–6). Throughout Samson's life, the Spirit of God rescued him from his own messes, yet Samson did not recognize God's help. He only saw his own desires and arrogantly thought that he alone controlled the results. Sadly, and too often just like Samson, we also lose sight of the fact that it is God doing the work in and through us. Working in our everyday life, God enables us to get up each morning, take a breath, and go about the business of the day. We think we are doing everything the right way; we have built this, we have accomplished that, or we believe that we have made our own success. In truth, God is the One who opens doors for us and allows the accomplishments. God gives us the ability to do the work that we do. He is the source of everything good in our lives. We certainly are not deserving of any merit for our success.

I have to say this, though: It is hard for strong people to stay humble. Yet, ironically, it is humility that brings strength, not the other way around. When we can balance humility and strength, God will use us in a powerful way. However,

God gives us the ability to do the work that we do.

the moment we begin to think our success is from our own efforts, God will allow lessons in our life to show us otherwise.

We will learn throughout this book that we need to leave our circumstances in God's hands. God's faithfulness has seen us through this far, and it is His faithfulness that will take us to the end. Despite what Samson thought about his own abilities, Scripture reminds us over and over again that it was the Spirit of God who accomplished Samson's feats, not Samson.

Paul tells us in the book of Philippians that God will complete the good work He began in us (Philippians 1:6). By His goodness and grace, we have the ability to grow in His strength and knowledge—in spite of who we are and what we have done. When God first created the world, it was without form and void. But by His Spirit, He brought forth light and life. Even in the midst of our failures, the Spirit of

God is able to bring order, peace, and light to our life. The moment we repent and turn to Christ, He can restore and redeem our ruin—even for those of us who are seemingly without form and void!

Samson Ran from God's Will

Samson was always running away from the call of God upon his life. We also have a tendency to run away from the responsibilities that God has asked us to handle. It might be in our home, in business, or in how we approach the stress of life. Let's face it—it's easy for some of us to run away from what God is calling us to do. Our natural instinct as human beings is to feed our rebellious flesh and not be obedient to what we know we should do. We like the feeling of being in control when we do things our way. As we study Samson's choices, maybe

We like the feeling of being in control when we do things our way.

we will be inspired to rethink our habit of feeding our controlling nature. God wants us to face reality, not run from it the way Samson did.

The Spirit of God faithfully came upon Samson, and the Lord showed him repeatedly what His will was for Samson's life, even to the point of vindicating him and giving him power. We first see this in the incident with Samson's marriage. He was planning to marry a forbidden Philistine woman. But God would intervene. Judges 14:4 tells us that the Lord *"was seeking an occasion to move against the Philistines."* God would save Samson from his own desire. But Samson didn't want God's will. Is that our attitude toward God as well? The Lord has possibly spoken to us for years about the things He wants to do in our lives, and He has asked us to be separate from the world and to be sanctified before Him. He wants a loving relationship with us—something far greater than anything we could ever enjoy on this earth. This is why He refers to Himself as a *"jealous God"* (Exodus 20:5). He doesn't want to share our attention or affection with other idols—our career, our car, our house, or even our kids. The things of this world constantly pull us away from Him, and oftentimes we feel like we can't find our way back. In this case, we are out of God's will. Just keep in mind that it is far better for us to be in the will of God while picking up trash than to be a billionaire living out of God's will.

Samson was a Nazirite, and being one meant that he knew what God wanted for his life (Judges 13:5). But he refused to surrender to God's authority. He dishonored God, breaking every one of his Nazirite vows, and he disgraced his parents. Samson defiled his purity and flirted with the enemy—figuratively and literally. He knew that he should not be in the Philistines' country with the enemy. He knew that he should not be messing around with women of questionable repute. He knew that he shouldn't go to the vineyard, but he went anyway. Samson continually refused to obey what God wanted him to do.

What is God's will for our lives? What is God saying to us? I challenge you to refuse to be like Samson, to stop opposing God and to start doing what God wants you to do. God has a purpose and a plan for your life, and He wants to do wonderful things in and through you, but He cannot use someone who is unyielding, unsanctified, and unwilling to commit to Him. We each know what God has been saying to us individually—just as Samson did. Are we finally going to listen, or are we going to keep on running in rebellion? As the saying goes, we can run but we can't hide. Never is that more true than with God.

What Does God Want Us to Do?

As we read through God's Word, God states very clearly what He wants us to do and that He will help us do it. We could spend our whole lives just doing what the Lord has laid out in His Word and we would never have to worry about His will . . . we would already be living it!

Romans 12:1 reads, *"I beseech you therefore, brethren, by the mercies of God, that you present your bodies a living sacrifice, holy, acceptable to God, which is your reasonable service."* Here is Micah 6:8: *"He has shown you, O man, what is good; and what does the LORD require of you but to do justly, to love mercy, and to walk humbly with your God?"* And 1 Thessalonians 5:23 states, *"Now may the God of peace Himself sanctify you completely; and may your whole spirit, soul, and body be preserved blameless at the coming of our Lord Jesus Christ."*

Samson Resisted the Authority of God

Not only did Samson run from God, but he also resisted the authority of God. Samson didn't want anyone to tell him what to do. Sound familiar? We know we are to clock out, but we don't; we know we are to check in, but we don't; we know we are to call and tell somebody we're going to be late, but we don't. We humans do not like rules, so we do what we want to do.

Most of us are in denial that many problems are caused by our own inability to follow directions.

We have a natural propensity to rebel against authority and to despise being ordered to do things. Few of us truly understand that when we don't submit to authority, we will get into trouble. Most of us are in denial that many problems are caused by our own inability to follow directions. Relationships also can fail because of a lack of submitting to one another. Ephesians 5:21 tells us to submit *"to one another in the fear of God."*

God's plan for Samson was clear. God told him to separate himself unto the Lord, but instead, Samson chose to hang out with the Philistines. God told him not to go into the vineyard, but Samson went anyway. God told him not to touch anything that was dead, but Samson extended his hand into the carcass of a dead lion. Samson refused to listen to anyone, not even God. Samson had a mind and a will of his own. Sadly, too often in our society, that kind of attitude is celebrated. To have a mind of our own usually means to be against God. Frankly, that's foolish.

Do you challenge God's authority? Remember, when we resist the authority of those whom God has placed over us, we are actually resisting God. If we're going to love the Lord with all our heart, we need to be going God's way. I find it funny that we love to resist, but we hate being resisted. Maybe that's why most of us love dogs instead of cats. Dogs come on our command and greet us at the door, wagging their tail, ready to do whatever we ask. But a cat thinks only of itself. A cat does not appear on our command nor does it greet us at the door; it has a mind of its own. Cats only come when it benefits them, sort of like us with authority. We need to ask ourselves, are we more like a cat or a dog?

> *God has called us to follow Him. He hasn't called us to resist, to get angry, to fight, or to challenge Him.*

God has called us to follow Him. He hasn't called us to resist, to get angry, to fight, or to challenge Him. He doesn't want us to be aggressive with our boss, our spouse, our kids, or anyone else for that matter. We need to listen because the Spirit of God is speaking to us. It is that still, small voice that quickens our heart and speaks to us about what is right, drawing us closer to Him.

Crossing the Line

Samson Reacted

Samson ran from God and resisted His authority. Yet another dangerous thing that Samson continued to do was to react to circumstances and situations in ways that did not honor God. Samson always reacted in anger by trying to get even with anybody who had hurt him. This behavior cultivated a downward cycle of violence in his life. Samson's desire for revenge grew out of his inability to stay in control of himself and his reactions. Anger is natural; forgiveness, however, is supernatural and can only be accomplished through the Spirit of God.

It is always self-defeating to react out of anger, but that's exactly what Samson did. He didn't stop to think through a situation or look to God for an answer. Instead, he just reacted according to his feelings. Once again, he rejected God's ways. It's sad to find brothers and sisters in the Lord reacting to their feelings just as Samson did: "Well, he said this and she said that; he felt this, and she felt that; and they didn't do this, and they didn't do that!" All of a sudden, Satan has us reacting in anger and not obeying God's standards with our actions because we are caught up in our feelings—snapshots of Samson.

When the Holy Spirit controls us, we act differently. We respond instead of reacting. We seek God's way and look for His peace. We should respond in the same way that Jesus would. Just imagine if Jesus responded to us the way we react to people when we are upset and angry. The reason why so many problems exist in our earthly relationships is because we tend to react and overreact instead of responding appropriately in the Spirit. If Samson had been in a right relationship with the Lord, his life would have been far different. What about us? How are we reacting to the challenges in our life? Are we reacting like Samson or responding like Jesus?

If we want to have the life that God desires for us, we need to say goodbye to our fleshly life...

In our lives, we need to say goodbye to the authority-hating, reactive "Samson." He represents the flesh. If we want to have the life that God desires for us, we need to say goodbye to our fleshly life—today. Samson lived a wasted life, but it did not have to be that way. All he had to do was humble himself and stay true to the call of God upon his life. He was called to be a judge of Israel, but instead, he was judged by the world. Let that not be us.

This book is about deciding how to live. Do we want to live the Lord's way or continue to live our life according to Samson's way? We need to choose between living in the flesh or in the Spirit, remembering that the way of the transgressor is hard but *"the law of the LORD is perfect, converting the soul"* (Psalm 19:7).

As we look at Samson's life, let's purpose in our hearts to sincerely learn from his mistakes. Let's choose not to follow in Samson's footsteps so that when we reflect back on our life, we see a fruitful obedience to our God-given opportunities to serve Him. God's plan for Samson was clear; He has a plan for us as well. Jeremiah 29:11 tells us clearly: *"For I know the thoughts that I think toward you, says the LORD, thoughts of peace and not of evil, to give you a future and a hope."* Let us allow God to work in our life for His glory.

Points to Ponder:

- Am I running away from responsibilities that God has given me to keep?

- Do I challenge or resist God's authority?

- Do I *react* to situations and follow my feelings instead of *responding* according to God's Word?

Chapter 2

A MIRACULOUS AND MARVELOUS BEGINNING

"And the Angel of the LORD appeared to the woman and said to her, 'Indeed now, you are barren and have borne no children, but you shall conceive and bear a son. Now therefore, please be careful not to drink wine or similar drink, and not to eat anything unclean. For behold, you shall conceive and bear a son. And no razor shall come upon his head, for the child shall be a Nazirite to God from the womb; and he shall begin to deliver Israel out of the hand of the Philistines' " (Judges 13:3–5).

Barrenness

I find it interesting that some of the great biblical heroes such as Abraham, Isaac, and Jacob all had wives who were barren. Even the word itself, "barren," sounds sterile and empty. It brings to mind the desolation of the desert. In biblical times, to be barren was a shameful thing. If a woman did not produce a child, she was scorned and derided. Just think about the situation of these women for a moment. Here are three great men of the Old Testament, ready to pass down their seed to the next generation, but for some unknown reason, the wombs of each of their wives were dead.

It's bad enough that these scorned women were not able to physically give birth, especially in the culture of those times. In addition, however, their barrenness was totally out of their control. Neither she nor her husband could do anything to change things. There were no surrogate mothers or fertility treatments, and there weren't any infomercials to provide resources for them. Their only recourse was to pray for the Lord's mercy. And the Lord was faithful; He answered their desperate prayers. He made all three women's wombs fruitful.

What happens if the barrenness is not physical but spiritual? I have seen this so often in ministry— affecting both men and women alike. A wife finally gives her heart in full surrender to Jesus Christ. She is no longer fighting against the Lord and is now ready to serve her family, her church, and her community wholeheartedly. Then there's her husband, lying on the couch, watching TV, spiritually as dead as a doornail. Or maybe it's a husband who has heard God's voice and is now ready to surrender everything to God. He is giving his time, talents, and yes, even his tithe, in obedience to his Lord. But instead of his wife rejoicing in his newfound obedience, she is beside herself, uptight, and furiously out of control.

Those barren moments, those unexpected roadblocks to serving God, those impossible situations—all represent that horrible barren womb described in the Old Testament. Just like Sarah and the other women in the Old Testament who cried out, "Why God, why me?"—we also cry out the very same thing, "Why God, why? God, what are You doing?

There is nothing too hard for God to do. He can tear down any roadblock.

Why are You allowing these things to happen to me?" We humans all ask these questions when we see roadblocks or impossible situations pop up within or around us. How do we overcome these impossible situations? The answer is so simple. There is nothing too hard for God to do. He can tear down any roadblock. He can overcome any obstacle, and He can heal, just as He can fill any womb by His incredible, supernatural power.

We all like spiritual revelations, but many times we aren't so sure we want to learn the lessons that come with them. Samson loved having the Spirit of God do great things through him, but he refused to acknowledge they weren't a result of his own doing. Why did God remove the heavy rock from that tomb on Easter morning? Was it not to reveal His power over Satan? Why did Christ raise Lazarus from the dead? Was it not to reveal His power over death? Why did God allow Abram's wife Sarai to be barren? *"But Sarai was barren; she had no child"* (Genesis 11:30). Why did God allow Isaac's wife, Rebekah, to be barren? *"Now Isaac pleaded with the LORD for his wife, because she was barren"* (Genesis 25:21). Why did God allow Jacob's wife Rachel to be barren? *"And when the LORD saw that Leah was unloved, He opened her womb; but Rachel was barren"* (Genesis 29:31). God wanted to teach them all to trust Him. He intended, through each of them, to bring a very special child into this world in order to save the righteous seed. God knows what He is doing.

In each case, God brought forth children according to His timing. Sarah was grieved by her barrenness and carried that pain with her everywhere she went. But the Lord blessed Sarah, and she brought forth Isaac at the ripe old age of 90! God had told Abraham: *"I will bless her and also give you a son by her; then I will bless her, and she shall be a mother of nations; kings of peoples shall be from her"* (Genesis 17:16). In many instances, God chose to bless and use women who were barren. Although society scorned them, God looked upon these women with compassion and love.

In the book of Judges, God sees the barrenness of this woman, Samson's mother, and brings forth life. Scripture tells us, *"Even when we were dead in trespasses, [God] made us alive together with Christ"* (Ephesians 2:5). God can breathe upon and touch any type of barrenness in our life. We may think that circumstances are never going to change, but they can. God can breathe on our desert right now. He can touch those areas that are barren, and He can bring life back to each one of them. Just as He provided for the children of Israel in the wilderness with food, water, and direction, He will provide for us as well. If we trust Him and believe in His promises, He will provide for our needs.

The children of Israel wandered in the desert for 40 years. Although they witnessed the power of God, they had no desire to leave the wilderness and enter the Promised Land. They were selfish in their decisions. God told them to go, but they put themselves before His Word and His will. In the same way, we often choose to live in our own wilderness of selfishness rather than in God's perfect will. This is the state in which nonbelievers find themselves. They live in a spiritual wilderness, going around in circles and wondering what life is all about, searching for answers everywhere except in the Word of God. Until we arrive at the place where we understand that nothing will fill the emptiness in our heart like the love of God, we will always be searching.

The Way of Peace

The way to a peaceful and joyous life is so simple—following God's plan and purpose for our life, not our own. Proverbs 3:5–6 encourages us to *"lean not on your own understanding; in all your ways acknowledge Him, and He shall direct your paths."* To accomplish this, we must trust in the Lord with all our heart. And to trust wholeheartedly, our relationship with Him must be deeply personal.

Because of God, this woman in Judges 13 miraculously bears a son named Samson. From his conception, Samson is called by God to be a Nazirite, and eventually he is used by God to save Israel from the Philistines. Just as God had a plan for Samson, He also has a plan for each one of us.

God's Calling on Samson's Life

Samson was no ordinary boy. He had extraordinary gifts, enormous potential, and an eminent call upon his life. He was given tremendous possibilities, yet he lived a life of tragic consequences. God called Samson to be consecrated, or set apart, to Him with the purpose of serving Him and delivering Israel from its enemy the Philistines. Numbers 6:1–7 sheds light on the Nazirite vow:

> *Then the LORD spoke to Moses, saying, "Speak to the children of Israel, and say to them: 'When either a man or woman consecrates an offering to take the vow of a Nazirite, to separate himself to the LORD, he shall separate himself from wine and similar drink; he shall drink neither vinegar made from wine nor vinegar made from similar drink; neither shall he drink any grape juice, nor eat fresh grapes or raisins. All the days of his separation he shall eat nothing that is produced by the grapevine, from seed to skin. All the days of the vow of his separation no razor shall come upon his head; until the days are fulfilled for which he separated himself to the LORD, he shall be holy. Then he shall let the locks of the hair of his head grow. All the days that he separates himself to the LORD he shall not go near a dead body. He shall not make himself unclean even for his father or his mother, for his brother or his sister, when they die, because his separation to God is on his head.'"*

There are three important aspects of the Nazirite vow: **First, it had to be voluntary.** It had to be from the heart. The Nazirite vow was something that could not be forced; rather, it had to come from Samson's own personal conviction.

Second, it was for a purpose. When Samson made a Nazirite vow, he was dedicating his life to the Lord and therefore was putting himself in a position to fulfill God's purposes.

Third, it was to be symbolic. By having Samson stay away from anything that produced wine, God was ensuring that Samson would not be influenced by alcohol, but by His Spirit. The Spirit needed to control Samson, not alcohol or anything else. In addition, Samson was not to cut his hair, ever. Not cutting his hair was a symbol of his dedication to the Lord. It is important to remember that his strength was not in his hair, but in his commitment to God.

Interestingly, we only know of three persons in the Bible who were called to be Nazirites for their entire life: Samson, Samuel, and John the Baptist. Generally, the Nazirite vow was only taken for a specific period of time, usually no more than a few weeks to a few months. During the time of a specific period of sanctification, the one taking the vow would abstain from his normal lifestyle to outwardly show his dedication to God. In fact, it is believed that the city of Nazareth got its name from there being so many Nazirite priests in the city. However, Samson, Samuel, and, many believe, John the Baptist as well were called to be separated for the work of the Lord for their entire lives.

In 1 Samuel 1:11, Hannah vows to give her son to the service of the Lord, and she vows that *"no razor shall come upon his head."* Hannah promised that her son would be a Nazirite for life. Many believe that John the Baptist was also a Nazirite because Luke 1:15 states that John *"will be great in the sight of the Lord, and shall drink neither wine nor strong drink."*

Samson's Nazirite service was remarkable in many ways. First of all, he did not take the vow voluntarily. It was given to him before his birth. Second, his service was to be for the duration of his life. Finally, he eventually broke every one of the stipulations required of being a Nazirite in spite of his great beginnings.

Samson's Godly Parents

Why should we discuss Samson's parents, when Samson is whom this book is about? Let me answer that question with a golden nugget from God's Word. Remember what Jesus taught us about truth in the book of John: *"The truth shall make you free"* (John 8:32). Parents, we must read this carefully. We must stop blaming ourselves for our children's chosen lifestyle. We must stop fighting with our spouse over our children's spirituality. Samson's parents were great parents. They did everything right in raising this child for

God. Yet in spite of all their love and incredible sacrifices, Samson broke their hearts. He made horrible choices in his life. He disrespected his parents and rebelled against his God. What could his parents have done differently? Nothing! Absolutely nothing! His parents were not responsible for Samson's choices in life.

Jeremiah the prophet reveals one of the most incredible Scriptures in the Bible about personal responsibility. In the book of Jeremiah, he says, *"In those days they shall say no more: The fathers have eaten sour grapes, and the children's teeth are set on edge."* But every one shall die for his own iniquity; every man who eats the sour grapes, his teeth shall be set on edge" (Jeremiah 31:29–30). What Jeremiah states is true: "Every one shall die for his own iniquity." Samson had wonderful parents, and his parents set a godly example before him daily. Even so, Samson rebelled. How I wish more parents would understand their calling and not take on their children's actions as their responsibility.

We learn from Judges chapter 13 that Samson's parents were God-fearing. Judges 13:19 tells us they made offerings to the Lord, and 13:22 tells us they feared God's holiness. Their marriage is a good example of what a Christian marriage should be. They were loving and willing to give their very best to God, each other, and their son. They were governed by God and not by selfishness. They were called and commissioned by God to raise Samson.

A Great Marriage

A great marriage is based on honest communication and sharing the truth. The key is learning how to say exactly what is on your heart—nothing more and nothing less—in a truthful yet loving way. This is why I saw Samson's mother as unique. She was able to communicate to her husband everything that happened between her and the Angel of the LORD (Judges 13:6–8). This type of honesty can be hard to come by in today's society. Often our communication within relationships is based on not telling the truth. We have learned to bend the truth to selfishly protect our own interests—whether it is with our boss, our friends, our family, our

We have learned to bend the truth to selfishly protect our own interests

spouse, or even our children. Manoah, Samson's father, didn't challenge his wife or question her. Instead, he went right to God and prayed. Manoah trusted what his wife said and understood her spirituality.

We see a wonderful illustration of God's love through this couple. They were a great example for Samson to follow. The husband is committed to prayer, and the wife's faithfulness is blessed because God is going to take away her barrenness and shame. Together, they hoped to raise a godly child. Manoah and his wife didn't want to make any mistakes. They needed more information and guidance on how to raise Samson. It's a wonderful thing when couples seek the Lord together, praying, "God, we don't want to make a mistake at work, at home, or with our children. Show us, teach us, guide us, Lord, in what we should do." Part of raising a godly child is being a parent obedient to God.

"So the Angel of the LORD said to Manoah, 'Of all that I said to the woman let her be careful. She may not eat anything that comes from the vine, nor may she drink wine or similar drink, nor eat anything unclean. All that I commanded her let her observe'" (Judges 13:13–14). In this passage, God called Samson's mother to observe the Nazirite vow as well. By exemplifying a life of obedience, she will help Samson live out his calling and purpose before God. As parents, the greatest way we can teach our children about God is by living out our faith in obedience to the Lord. It's not, "Do as I say and not as I do," but rather, "Do as I do."

Worship Together

Judges 13:19–20 describes, "So Manoah took the young goat with the grain offering, and offered it upon the rock to the LORD. And He did a wondrous thing while Manoah and his wife looked on—it happened as the flame went up toward heaven from the altar—the Angel of the LORD ascended in the flame of the altar! When Manoah and his wife saw this, they fell on their faces to the ground."

As this Scripture indicates, this couple worshiped God together. Together they heard from God, saw God, and talked to God. There is nothing better than when a marriage exemplifies God's command of two becoming one flesh. My wife, Gail, and I have been married for nearly 40 years. The greatest times when we have seen the gifts of the Holy Spirit manifested are when we have come together in agreement as a couple to worship God, to serve the Lord, or to discipline our children. There were times when Gail and I would talk to our kids together, and it was clear that the Lord was using both of our gifts to get through to them.

I know that when a husband and wife come together to seek and worship God, good things are going to happen in life. When we start praying together for the ministry, for our children, or for other specific issues in our life, then God begins to move. Pentecost happened when everyone was in one accord. Therefore, the Bible says for husbands and wives to dwell together accordingly, lest their prayers be hindered (See 1 Peter 3:7). Because Samson's parents worshiped the Lord together, they experienced God's love in a miraculous way when He gave them a son.

Samson Is Born

Judges 13:24–25 narrates, *"So the woman bore a son and called his name Samson; and the child grew, and the LORD blessed him. And the Spirit of the LORD began to move upon him at Mahaneh Dan between Zorah and Eshtaol."*

Samson was a miracle child. His name actually means "sunny." His life starts out as a light. The Spirit of God was upon him and moved within him. Samson had a high calling from God and a clear purpose. He had godly and loving parents who trained him in the ways of the Lord. Not only was he a Nazirite, outwardly proclaimed by his hair, but he also had superhuman strength. Was he strong from birth, or did he develop his Superman-like strength as he grew? The Bible doesn't tell us. However, it is crystal-clear that Samson possessed supernatural strength as we read through his life in Judges chapters 13–16.

Imagine being entrusted to raise such an extraordinary child! Many parents feel that their children are extraordinarily gifted, and no doubt some of them are. But imagine having Samson as a son. His parents knew he was special. After all, an angel announced his birth and prophesied great things to come from his life. His parents may also have treated him differently. Were they extra strict due to the high expectations on his life? Or were they permissive, treating him with kid gloves? How did Samson perceive his call and gifts from God? We don't know. We do know, however, that as an adult, Samson was reluctant to fulfill the God-given challenges before him. He did not respect or obey his parents' counsel, and his boldness and personal confidence were undeniable.

Samson had a lot of potential. He was called from birth, bestowed with spiritual and physical gifts, and spiritually prepared for the tasks before him from a very young age. We will see in the following chapters, however, how the light that Samson started out with slowly began to fade. Rebellion and lust end up rearing their ugly heads in Samson's life. Will he succumb to sin, or will he be obedient to God?

A High Cost to Low Living

This story reminds us that there is a high cost to low living. When we desire to live a Christian life with one foot in the world and one foot in the Spirit, it will cost us much. We will make bad decisions resulting in some tragic consequences and then find ourselves more in the world than in Christ. Samson could not have asked for a more wonderful beginning in life. Yet, as we will see, Samson wasted his miraculous and marvelous beginning. He lived a wasted life because he chose to live for himself out of pure selfishness instead of through obedience fulfilling God's purpose for him in this world.

Points to Ponder:

- What are the barren areas of my life that I need to let God fill and make fruitful?
- What are my unique gifts?
- Am I seeking to know what God wants me to do for Him?

Chapter 3

LUST AT FIRST SIGHT

"Now Samson went down to Timnah, and saw a woman in Timnah of the daughters of the Philistines. So he went up and told his father and mother, saying, 'I have seen a woman in Timnah of the daughters of the Philistines; now therefore, get her for me as a wife.' Then his father and mother said to him, 'Is there no woman among the daughters of your brethren, or among all my people, that you must go and get a wife from the uncircumcised Philistines?' And Samson said to his father, 'Get her for me, for she pleases me well' " (Judges 14:1–3).

A Vital Lesson

If we could learn just one lesson from the story of Samson, it would be this: Samson made selfish choices, and consequently, the situations in which he found himself were of his own making, not God's. So often, Satan lies to us and tells us that God doesn't care about our circumstances. He will whisper in our ear, "If God loved you, then why are you stuck with this spouse?" or "If God loved you, then why are you in debt?" Yet the reality is that God's Holy Spirit warned us about the relationship we are in beforehand, but we wouldn't listen. God spoke to us about not spending excessively, but we just had to have that car or that house and we wouldn't listen. Too often we make choices based on how we feel rather than on what God commands. Samson made horrible choices, and they cost him dearly. Although Samson is considered an eternal man of faith today, he was not a consistently faithful man to God when he was alive. Neither was he faithful to his parents or his people until the last few minutes of his life.

Too often we make choices based on how we feel rather than on what God commands.

We need to pay attention to this lesson because it is possible to have the gift of God and to be inspired by the Lord, yet not to be faithful to Him. This is exactly why I encourage believers to stay in fellowship with the Lord. We must stay in His Word, stay in prayer, be accountable to fellow believers, and serve others. Once any of these connections are broken, our sinful nature, as well as the Enemy, can creep in and do all kinds of damage.

The Danger of Living Too Close to Sin

"Now Samson went down to Timnah, and saw a woman in Timnah of the daughters of the Philistines" (Judges 14:1).

In this Scripture, the very first words read, "Now Samson went down. . . ." Boy, what a testimony of his life. When we walk away from what God wants, we do the same thing as Samson—we'll go down. Remember Jonah? He went down too. Instead of doing what God wanted, Jonah went down to Tarshish; he went down to Joppa; he went down to the ship; he went down to the bottom of the ship; he went down to the belly of the fish; and finally, he went down to the bottom of the ocean. In other words, Jonah was "going down" because he turned away from God.

As we dive into the downfall of Samson's life, we discover his problem with lust. Samson had all the power and physical strength given to him by the Lord, but he had no purity in his heart. Lust is defined as "a bodily appetite for pleasure," and it can come in many forms. One can strongly desire alcohol, drugs, food, or gambling, to name a few strongholds. In Samson's case, lust refers to sexual desire. He spent days and even years allowing himself to be seduced by Philistine women. His vow of separation from the world and dedication to the Lord was long forgotten as he sought one pretty face and body after another.

It's interesting that the tribe of Dan was next to the city of the Philistines (just four miles away). That was a problem. Oftentimes we get too close to sin. The tribe of Dan was too close to the Philistines, and it became a wicked tribe within the children of Israel. When we, as God's children, begin to look upon and then to mingle with unbelievers, we start to act like them. Over time, we accept their attitudes, adhere to their values, and adapt to their lifestyles. This can be seen in the life of Jacob. He lived too close to Shechem, the Canaanite city that was devoted to pagan gods. Jacob's intermingling resulted in the rape of his daughter Dinah, as well as the murderous acts of two of his sons, Simeon and Levi. Why are we so easily tempted and led astray? Why are we not content with the things God has given us? We are tempted because sin appears to be so much more exciting. Yet that perceived excitement is just a wicked deception.

In the story of Adam and Eve, the forbidden fruit looked good and smelled good. Like Adam and Eve, we begin to think that if we just take a little bite, we'll be enlightened. *Go ahead*, we think to ourselves, *no one will ever know. Come on, it's just a piece of fruit. Did God really say not to eat it? Are we sure He said that? We have worked hard. We deserve it.* Sound familiar? It's the same old argument from the beginning of time. Just as Eve was deceived in the Garden of Eden, so are we. We spend so much of our time looking at and lusting after things, debating with ourselves and God about them, that we find ourselves completely drained. We have been robbed spiritually—and don't even know it.

Because of his constant sinning, Samson did not know that the Spirit of God had left him. Samson regularly resisted the Spirit of the living God. He repeatedly quenched the Spirit. Samson grieved the Holy Spirit and was not willing to yield or surrender to His leading.

Samson was in the wrong country looking at the wrong things. He had no business being there. He was checking out the Philistine women who worshiped foreign gods. He was even looking at the possibility of marrying one of these women. So right from the beginning, Samson was knowingly breaking his Nazirite vows. He was now in a place where he shouldn't be and was considering things he should have been avoiding altogether. Does that sound like us? Shouldn't we be constantly asking ourselves why we are in certain places and what we are doing? Sometimes, as believers, we end up where we ought not to be. That is when we start to take the first step downward.

We have walked off course and are no longer walking in the power of the Holy Spirit.

We must listen to God, not to our own desires. When the Holy Spirit asks us, "What are you doing here?" He already knows the answer to the question. He is asking us to reveal our heart so we can confess before Him that He is right and we are wrong. We have walked off course and are no longer walking in the power of the Holy Spirit. God is putting a caution sign within our heart to reveal our innermost feelings. When this happens to us, do we listen to God, or are we so distracted by our selfishness that we can't hear Him?

In 1 Kings 19:9, God asked Elijah the very same question, *"What are you doing here, Elijah?"* Elijah responded, *"I alone am left; and they seek to take my life."* What a selfish thing to say to God! God responded, in essence, to His servant Elijah, "I have seven thousand who have not bowed their knee to other gods. Why are you so discouraged?" Elijah had taken his eyes off the Lord and put them on his own situation. Conversely, we need to stay in constant fellowship with God. He will continue to speak to us and lead us in His still, small voice. Constant distractions and discouragement will prevent us from hearing His voice. That is when we—like Samson— begin to follow our own desires down a path to destruction.

Samson was in terrible danger at this point because he was living not by faith but by sight. Samson saw what he wanted and took it. He was living for the sole purpose of fulfilling the pleasures of his flesh. He was trying to satisfy the here and now. Samson was not living with any trust or hope in God, nor did he have any desire to do so.

Samson Makes a Wrong Choice

"So he went up and told his father and mother, saying, 'I have seen a woman in Timnah of the daughters of the Philistines; now therefore, get her for me as a wife' " (Judges 14:2).

Samson didn't say anything to his parents but, "Get her for me." I can imagine that, at that moment, Samson's parents were brokenhearted. As many Christian parents know, our kids often want the blessings of our God, but not God Himself. I can almost hear his parents cry out to him, "Samson, do you understand what you're about to do? Son, we didn't raise you this way; what about your covenant with God?" But like many of our children today, Samson did not listen.

God gave Samson, as He gives all of us, free will. Samson had the ability to make choices. Samson did not want what his parents had nor did he want to submit to their authority. He did not want what God wanted for him. His mind was set on doing what he wanted to do, and he was deceived by his own selfishness and pride. Samson knew that he was special and that he had tremendous strength. He thought that having these special abilities gave him a license to live any way he wanted. Because God didn't deal with him immediately, Samson assumed it was okay to do what he was doing. Samson misinterpreted his own free will as God's permissiveness. Sadly, he was going to pay a very high price for his rebellion.

Too often, when we are living in rebellion, we still experience God's blessing upon our lives and think everything is okay in our relationship with the Lord, when in reality, it is not. Rather, it is God sending us a message that He's alive and well and He wants us to turn around. He's not endorsing what we are doing but is giving us a chance to repent. I believe that many people are going down this road thinking that it's permissible to live in sin because they are enjoying success and rich blessings. We should not mistake God's grace for His longsuffering. Even though the Lord desires that we turn away from sin immediately, He will grant us a season to learn the importance of a life of repentance. Just because God doesn't judge or deal with our sin immediately does not mean that He is approving of our actions. We will eventually reap what we sow. When we believe that we are getting away with sin, we give birth to the idea that we are above not only other people,

> *We should not mistake God's grace for His longsuffering.*

but the Word of God as well. Yes, He is our loving Father and wants to bless us, but we also must be thankful for His grace, repent, and live a life that is pleasing to Him.

Samson regularly reveals his lack of character by demonstrating his inability to fulfill his Nazirite vow. We see this in marriages today too. Couples make a vow on their wedding day "to have and to hold, for richer, for poorer, till death do us part." Then, when the honeymoon ends and life becomes routine, the question becomes, will they stick it out through the good times and the bad? Sadly, many times this answer is found in the actions and choices couples make. God is going to use Samson's wrong choices to break the Philistines, to achieve His higher purpose, and to destroy the enemy. Of course, Samson's choices are not without personal consequences. God will also discipline him.

Eventually, Samson walked away from everything godly he had been taught and found himself on the verge of fulfilling his lustful heart. This is what happens when we walk away from God. This is what happens when our children walk away from the Lord. What they are really saying is, "I do not want your God, and I do not want you to have authority over my life." Judges 14:4 reads, *"But his father and mother did not know that it was of the LORD—that He was seeking an occasion to move against the Philistines. For at that time the Philistines had dominion over Israel."* Samson was clearly acting outside of the will of God, yet Scripture tells us that although Samson was doing evil, God was going to turn the table and use this evil for His glory.

Walking into the Face of Temptation

"So Samson went down to Timnah . . . and came to the vineyards of Timnah. Now to his surprise, a young lion came roaring against him" (Judges 14:5).

Samson continued in his downward spiral. Where did he go this time? He went down to a vineyard. Now, remember, as a Nazirite, he made a vow never to drink wine or to eat raisins or grapes. So why in the world was he walking among the grape vineyards? That would be like taking a guy who has a problem with promiscuous lust to a party at the Playboy mansion. Why would a person do that? We need to be careful of the carnal curiosity that deceives us into thinking, "I'm spiritually strong. I won't be tempted. I won't sin. I'm just looking." Samson was now walking right into the face of temptation. He was flirting with it as if it were a game. He, no doubt, was saying to himself, "I can handle this. I can walk in this vineyard. I'm not even going to touch a grape." What foolishness.

Once again, Samson was somewhere he shouldn't be. So what did God do? God sent a lion. God wanted to turn Samson away from the vineyard, so He put a roadblock in his way: a large, snarling, you'd-better-turn-back roadblock. It's likely we've all experienced roadblocks in our life. These kinds of roadblocks stop us dead in our tracks, and we hear that still, small voice telling us, "You better not do that." I know I've experienced this. God uses many "lions" in our life—to warn us, to stop us, and to check our hearts. But too often, we don't listen. Instead, we drown out that voice of God just as Samson did.

Then, like Samson, we begin to break one vow after another. How could Samson keep walking away from God? How does anyone walk away from the Lord? It happens when we start breaking one vow, one commandment at a time. It's a process, not a single event. We go where we shouldn't go. We look at something we shouldn't see. It's a dangerous place to be. In our heart, we are defying God. We are saying to God, "Listen, I know what You want from me, but I'm not going to give it to You. I appreciate how You want to bless me, but I'm not going to obey You this time."

We often hear that Satan comes after those who are right with God, but I can assure you that Satan also comes after those who are disobedient toward God. Satan wins them over and beats them down. The more disobedient we are, the louder the lion's roar becomes. God wanted to turn Samson away from the vineyard. He was in the wrong place. The young lion roared, and God gave Samson plenty of opportunity to make the right choice, to repent, to turn around and go back to where he belonged. Instead, Samson used his gift of great strength and beat down the roaring lion. This would have been great if it were the Lord's will, but out of His will, it was tragic.

Samson Conceals His Sin

"And the Spirit of the LORD came mightily upon him, and he tore the lion apart as one would have torn apart a young goat, though he had nothing in his hand. But he did not tell his father or his mother what he had done" (Judges 14:6).

This Scripture states that Samson did not tell his parents what he had done. Why didn't he tell his mom and dad? He didn't tell them because he didn't want to hear them say that what he did was wrong. When we do something wrong or when we go someplace we shouldn't, we rarely tell people. Thus begins our secret life. We begin to have double standards because we can't afford for anybody to know what is really going on in our life. There is a common saying that I have heard, "You are only as sick as your secrets." When all our energy is going toward protecting our sinful life and keeping our secrets in the dark, then there can never be healing or freedom—only entrapment. Satan lies and tells us to hide in the darkness. Secret sins, however, keep us from fellowship with God and imprison us within our own hearts and minds. The book of James says that when we confess our sins one to another and pray for one another, then we can be healed (James 5:16). When we are willing to live our life in the light, His light, then all darkness flees and we are set free. Knowing this, Samson still chose to keep his sins a secret.

Secret sins are evident throughout the Bible—from the lowest to the mightiest of men. Remember young Joseph with the coat of many colors? In the book of Genesis, Joseph's brothers, due to jealousy and hatred, sold him into slavery and lied to their father, claiming that Joseph was killed by a wild animal. Joseph's brothers were in bondage to their secret lie for nearly 20 years. Or consider King David. For a year, he kept the secret of his adulterous affair with Bathsheba and the murder of her husband, Uriah. It sapped his strength, and he was unfruitful (Psalm

Secret sins keep us from fellowship with God and imprison us within our own hearts and minds.

32). What a burden we carry when we keep secrets in an attempt to protect ourselves from judgment and punishment. The problem lies not in our desiring to keep secrets from people, but in forgetting that God already knows all about them. Do we really think we can keep anything from God? Keeping secret sins weighs us down and prevents us from being carefree. Rather than having a light heart, free from the weight of sin, we are weighed down by the heavy burdens of guilt, shame, and iniquity.

For Samson, the incident with the lion became a very private, sinful moment in his life. He couldn't look his parents in the eyes and say to them, "I am violating God." The Spirit of God had come upon Samson to deliver him, not for him to rip the lion apart. The lion was unclean. Samson could have simply turned away, but instead, he chose to violate God's law again and touch that which was unclean. The incident didn't end there, however. Samson went back to the scene of the crime to pridefully marvel at what he had done.

The Lure and Pull of Sin

"After some time, when he returned to get her, he turned aside to see the carcass of the lion. And behold, a swarm of bees and honey were in the carcass of the lion" (Judges 14:8).

Even though it was God who had delivered him, Samson was constantly lusting over the power that came upon him and thinking about what he had done to the lion. No doubt, every night, every morning, every waking hour, he was thinking about going back. The lure, the pull, and the excitement of sin were drawing him back to the vineyard, back to the Philistine woman, and back to the carcass of the lion. In humans, there is a tremendous lust toward evil, and

Samson is an example of what happens when we allow that lust to control us. Satan was pushing Samson to do that which was wrong before the Lord. Samson thought he was just having fun, but he was unknowingly being used by the Enemy.

Perhaps we can relate to Samson. Maybe we have a tremendous pull in our own life. We have to go to the Internet. We have to push just one more button for one more site to look at. We have to smoke that one last little joint. We have to have one more drink, and that last one puts us into full-on bondage. We need God to cleanse our mind and our heart. We have to understand that God forbids what we are doing and that God's Word is the only thing that can cleanse a human heart and conscience. All Samson needed to do was to turn to God and trust His Word, but the pull of Satan's lie was much more exciting to Samson than the will of God.

"He took some of it in his hands and went along, eating. When he came to his father and mother, he gave some to them, and they also ate. But he did not tell them that he had taken the honey out of the carcass of the lion" (Judges 14:9).

Samson was headed deeper into his destruction. He had put his hand inside a filthy carcass and took out honey, defiling himself and breaking his vow to the Lord. Samson's parents were godly people; his mother had taken the same vow as her son. Yet here was Samson, offering his mother defiled honey. Not only did Samson violate his own vow, but now his mother, who had lived a holy and pure life, was also defiled by her son's actions. Samson's sin blinded and deceived his mother too. That's what sin does. It hurts not only us, but those around us as well. When we are only thinking about ourselves and our own needs or desires, we don't think about how our actions will affect others. Our selfishness blinds us into focusing only on fulfilling this desire. We think, "Nobody has to know about it. Nobody will get hurt." We're not thinking about others. We're not thinking about consequences. We're not thinking, period. We're only chasing after our lust, to the detriment of all.

> *When we are only thinking about ourselves... we don't think about how our actions will affect others.*

Samson ignored all of the roadblocks God created and continued to seek his own will. He desired to marry a Philistine woman, and despite his parents' pleading, he continued on with his wedding plans. Samson even went through with the wedding ceremony, although the marriage was not consummated. Still boasting in his sin, Samson posed a riddle to the guests at his wedding feast. The riddle was based on his extraordinary feat against the lion in the vineyard and the honey inside the dead carcass. He was sure it was unsolvable. For three days, the men could not unravel the riddle. Eventually, they went to Samson's wife and forced her to get the answer from her husband. Finally, after her continual pressing, Samson explained his riddle to her, and she in turn told the Philistines. This ignited Samson's anger.

God Continually Rescues Samson

"Then the spirit of the LORD came upon him mightily, and he went down to Ashkelon and killed thirty of their men, took their apparel, and gave the changes of clothing to those who had explained the riddle. So his anger was aroused, and he went back up to his father's house. And Samson's wife was given to his companion, who had been his best man" (Judges 14:19–20).

Samson went down to Ashkelon with anger as his motive. Things were falling apart in his life, and he was out of control. Samson ended up killing 30 Philistines and then throwing their bloody garments at those who had solved the riddle that he had challenged.

God certainly had His hands full when it came to Samson. Tragically, in his whole life, Samson never did anything for God or fulfilled God's will. Isn't that one of the saddest statements that can be made about someone? Samson was busy doing things, but not for God or for His kingdom. The Lord was continually rescuing Samson from himself and from the enemy. Instead of him and God fighting the enemy together, Samson was consistently fighting against God. Sometimes we think we're fighting for God, but in reality we find that we're really fighting against God. Too often we think God doesn't care or is even cruel because He takes things away from us. In reality, God loves us and is protecting us from people, things, or circumstances that will destroy us.

Many people today, Christians and non-Christians alike, are angry with God because of some difficult moment in their life. They believe God has let them down or that He just doesn't care about them. Nothing could be further from the truth. God loves us with an everlasting love; His love for us is irreversible and unconditional. In the book of Romans, chapter 8, Paul the apostle tells us that nothing can separate us from the love of God. In the very same chapter, Paul exhorts us, *"If God is for us, who can be against us?"* There's one more golden nugget in the eighth chapter of Romans: *"Who shall bring a charge against God's elect? . . . Who is he who condemns? It is Christ who died . . . who is even at the right hand of God, who also makes intercession for us."* In essence, Christ died for us, and there is no longer any guilt. If we believe anything other than or contrary to these Scriptures, then we are being lied to by our Enemy—the roaring lion.

Samson, in the midst of his rage, finally ended up going home to his father's house. Isn't it interesting that God knows how to get us home when we are in trouble? That's where we need to be in those times—in our heavenly Father's house. Everything that's happening in our life right now is to get us home. All the disappointments, the agonies, the times that we've been caught doing things we shouldn't have being doing, all the bad relationships, all the lost jobs and aimless moves—these all have served the purpose of getting us to our Father's house. God is our loving Father and has a plan for our life. Left to ourselves, we are going to blow it. If you are in turmoil as you're reading this, give in—go to your Father's house. He's waiting for you.

We need to understand that God sends His Spirit to rescue us out of the hands of the Enemy so that we will be able to do the work that God wants us to do. We need to stop fighting with God and trying to justify our actions. We need to do what the Lord has asked us to do—to pray, to stay in the Word, and to get involved in serving His people. When we follow the Lord's direction for our life, we find that our lives are filled with joy, purpose, and fullness.

Points to Ponder:

- Do I make selfish choices that leave me with undesirable consequences?
- Are there any secret areas in my heart on which God needs to shed His light?
- Am I carrying around anger or unconfessed bitterness in my heart toward God because of circumstances within my life?

Chapter 4

THE FRUIT OF REVENGE

"Then Samson went and caught three hundred foxes; and he took torches, turned the foxes tail to tail, and put a torch between each pair of tails. When he had set the torches on fire, he let the foxes go into the standing grain of the Philistines, and burned up both the shocks and the standing grain, as well as the vineyards and olive groves. Then the Philistines said, 'Who has done this?' And they answered, 'Samson, the son-in-law of the Timnite, because he has taken his wife and given her to his companion.' So the Philistines came up and burned her and her father with fire. Samson said to them, 'Since you would do a thing like this, I will surely take revenge on you, and after that I will cease' " (Judges 15:4–7).

Cause and Effect

We've all heard the phrase "cause and effect." Although this exact phrase is not found in the Bible, its principles and concepts are found throughout Scripture. The word, "cause," is all about what we do, how we do it, and why we do it. The word, "effect," refers to the results or consequences of what we do. God stated it even better when He said, *"Whatever a man sows, that he will also reap"* (Galatians 6:7).

I remember the first time I heard this phrase used about me. I was at my friend Paul's house, who just happens to be a brilliant lawyer. We were talking about the church, and I told him about a decision I was going to make. He just gazed at me with one of those puzzling looks, like in a courtroom setting. I asked him what was going on inside that lawyer's mind of his, but I wasn't sure it would be encouraging. I was wrong. Paul said, "Pastor Steve, whenever you make a decision, you set in

Make sure you think things through first before you make a decision.

motion cause and effect. If you make a decision concerning someone on your staff, your decision affects not only that person, but also his or her family, as well as you and the church. So make sure it is a great decision." I got his point. He continued, "If you go out and get drunk, for example, you might think you have a reason or cause to do it, but the effect will be overwhelming to you and devastating to those around you. You will lose everything God has given to you and mar your character for life, possibly even go to jail. Make sure you think things through first before you make a decision."

What great insight and a principle for life. If we rob a bank, we will go to jail. If we hang out with gangs, we will more than likely get shot. In this chapter, we will explore the lesson of cause and effect lived out in the life of Samson. It is also a clear message on the problem of revenge. Taking matters into our own hands produces consequences: cause and effect.

Revenge Is Natural

Revenge is a part of our fleshly, sinful nature. It is selfishness and pride in action. When someone hurts us or takes something away from us, our natural response is to want to get even. We want to strike back and hurt them just as they have hurt us.

As we look into Judges 15, we see that revenge begets revenge. It reads in verse 2 that Samson came back to see his wife, but her father had given his daughter to another man. The father, no doubt, was seeking revenge on Samson for all the problems he had caused. Because Samson felt he had been tricked, he now planned to get even.

In verse 5, Samson went out and burned the Philistine crops. He caught 300 foxes, tied their tails together, stuck a torch in between the rope holding their tails, and set them loose to burn all the fields of the Philistines. When the Philistines saw what Samson had done, they turned quickly to revenge their losses as well. Their anger was out of control and they did something that is hard to believe, yet it happens too often in our world. They acted out their revenge by burning Samson's wife and her father. Revenge begets revenge at a terrible price.

When Samson found out what the Philistines had done, as to be expected, he returned to seek his vengeance. He went out, found some men, knocked them over the head, and slaughtered them. Sadly enough, Samson was no better than the heathen, even though he had God on his side. He allowed his anger to consume him and now began to murder people. Samson's anger was progressive. He first took some helpless animals and used them to set the Philistine fields on fire; his next step was to kill numerous human beings. Sin is always progressive. It will start with a seed, turn into a thought, and finally explode into an action.

The story doesn't end there. Samson and the Philistines continued to seek revenge against one another all the way to the end of Samson's life. Simply put, there is no end to revenge; it will never be satisfied. Just look at what's currently happening in the Middle East. Palestine attacks Israel, Israel counterattacks the Palestinians, and then the Palestinians counter Israel's counterattack. It's a constant cycle of attack, retribution, and counterattack. There's no stopping the course of revenge once it has been engaged.

The same vicious cycle of getting even also happens in a church, in a marriage, and in a single person's life. Yet God is looking to bless the person who is willing to die to himself, allowing himself to be vulnerable and to say, "I am willing to stop this cycle and allow myself to be hurt (or cheated), if that's what is required to bring peace." That's what Jesus did on the cross. He shed His glory. He allowed Himself to be brutalized and tortured for our sins. He became totally vulnerable, hanging naked and bloody on the cross so that we might find peace. He became a son so we might become the sons of God. He became poor so that we might become rich in Him. He became sin so we might become righteous. And He became a servant so that we might become kings and priests forever. Philippians 2:8 describes Jesus' actions so beautifully: *"And being found in appearance as a man, He humbled Himself and became obedient to the point of death, even the death of the cross."* This was the ultimate act of selflessness and what should have brought peace to all, but sadly, not all accept His sacrifice.

Vengeance belongs to God. The only way we can stop the vicious cycle of getting even is in the name of the Lord. We need to die to who we are and let God fight our battles. We need to believe that God is able to vindicate, justify, and sanctify our life. Psalm 94:1 says, *"O LORD God, to whom vengeance belongs—O God, to whom vengeance belongs, shine forth!"* We need to trust that God will repay those who do us evil. We must remember what God said in His Word—that He will make even evil praise him. Joseph said to his brothers in Genesis 50:20: *"But as for you, you meant evil against me; but God meant it for good, in order to bring it about as it is this day, to save many people alive."* Scripture makes clear that the job of revenge does not belong to us; it belongs to God, who does all things righteous and just. Romans 12:19 says, *"Beloved, do not avenge yourselves, but rather give place to wrath; for it is written, 'Vengeance is Mine, I will repay,' says the Lord."*

It's Not Just a Matter of Getting Even

"*You have heard that it was said, 'An eye for an eye and a tooth for a tooth.' But I tell you not to resist an evil person. But whoever slaps you on your right cheek, turn the other to him also*" (Matthew 5:38–39).

Our natural tendency, however, is to say, "If you pluck out my eye, I'm going to pop both of your eyes out. You hit me in the face, and I'm going to smack you back in the face and knock your teeth out!" Let's face it, we look out for ourselves, so when somebody hurts us, our selfish flesh nature doesn't want to just get even; it wants to do greater harm and hurt them worse than they hurt us. We want to one-up them and teach the culprit a lesson. When this happens, we tend to think, "*Who are you to violate me? Do you think you are better than me? I'll show you who's in control.*" However, the Bible says in Philippians 2:3, "Let nothing be done through selfish ambition or conceit, but in lowliness of mind let each esteem others better than himself."

When someone uses us or hurts us, we see just how quickly the ugly monster of selfishness can rise in us!

Now, we might think we have a wonderful heart, but we don't. The Bible says that we have a wicked and perverse heart. The apostle Paul said it best, "In me (that is, in my flesh) nothing good dwells" (Romans 7:18). The only goodness in our life is Jesus Christ. When someone uses us or hurts us, we see just how quickly the ugly monster of selfishness can rise in us! When we have been hurt, cheated, or offended, all of a sudden selfishness explodes inside our heart and our emotions are quickly out of control. Therein lies the real danger because now we have the capacity to really do some major damage to someone, even those we love the most.

James 4:1–3 reads, *"Where do wars and fights come from among you? Do they not come from your desires for pleasure that war in your members? You lust and do not have. You murder and covet and cannot obtain. You fight and war. Yet you do not have because you do not ask. You ask and do not receive, because you ask amiss, that you may spend it on your pleasures."* James is clarifying that when we fight, war, and want to get even, we are lusting after the flesh and grieving the Holy Spirit. We need to stop.

How Do We React When We Are Blindsided

What caused the downward spiral of revenge in Samson's life? We might say a woman scorned, or in this case, a father-in-law scorned. When Samson, in a fit of rage, left the young woman who was to be his wife, her father already had it in his mind that she was not going to marry Samson. But Samson came back for her because in his mind they were married, although they had not consummated the marriage. When he came back it was the time of harvest, so he brought a young goat with him. Judges 15:1–2 explains, *"After a while, in the time of wheat harvest, it happened that Samson visited his wife with a young goat. And he said, 'Let me go in to my wife, into her room.' But her father would not permit him to go in. Her father said, 'I really thought that you thoroughly hated her; therefore I gave her to your companion. Is not her younger sister better than she? Please, take her instead.'"*

The father had watched his daughter cry for seven days while Samson called her names and then in anger went out and killed 30 of his Philistine friends. I believe this father was so angry at Samson that he had decided to take things into his own hands. He tried to take control of the situation in order to solve his daughter's problem. So in one quick decision, he gave his daughter to another man. This made Samson angry—really, really angry.

Manoah, Samson's father, had paid for everything and made all of the arrangements for the marriage. Technically speaking, the Philistine woman really should have been Samson's wife, but it wasn't God's will for them to be married in the first place. In fact, Samson was completely out of God's will by now, and he simply didn't care. But God cared, and once again, His mercy and grace saved Samson from his horrible rebellion. If Samson had married this woman, it would have been the end of his ministry. So God, in His wonderfully gracious way, was protecting His selfish servant from the foolishness of his own poor decisions. In the same way, God many times needs to intervene in our circumstances so that we do not make tragic mistakes in our life, and He does it even when He knows we'll believe He is wrong.

The important lesson to learn here is that sometimes we invest our life, our talent, our time, and our finances and then all of a sudden things don't go according to our plan.

Revenge is natural, but forgiveness is supernatural.

Samson was blindsided by his father-in-law's decision to give his wife to another man. He was hurt and devastated. How do we react when we are blindsided? What do we do when God decides to take us a different way than the way we wanted to go? Are we going to be wise enough to look to God and see what He's doing in our life, or like Samson, are we going to burn with revenge and a desire to get even?

Forgiveness Is Supernatural

Matthew 18:21–22 reads, *"Then Peter came to Him and said, 'Lord, how often shall my brother sin against me, and I forgive him? Up to seven times?' Jesus said to him, 'I do not say to you, up to seven times, but up to seventy times seven.'"* Jesus' point is to not keep count at all, but to be continually willing to forgive.

Revenge is natural, but forgiveness is supernatural. Peter thought that he was being generous to forgive someone seven times, but Jesus, in one quick moment, humbled poor Peter by letting him know that forgiveness needs to be unlimited. Forgiveness is not so much an action as it is an attitude. Our natural heart wants to defend ourselves, to get even and strike back when we've been hurt. However, granting forgiveness is the work of the Holy Spirit. Being unforgiving, holding resentment, being bitter, or talking about getting even are signs that the Spirit of the living God is not doing a work in our heart and that He is being quenched. Mark 11:25–26 exhorts, *"And whenever you stand praying, if you have anything against anyone, forgive him, that your Father in heaven may also forgive you your trespasses. But if you do not forgive, neither will your Father in heaven forgive your trespasses."*

I once read a story about a truck driver who wanted to get a cup of coffee and breakfast. He pulled the truck up in front of a diner and went inside to eat. Three burly bikers came in to the diner and started mouthing off. They saw the truck driver sitting at the counter, so they walked up to him, took his plate of food, and threw it in his face. They mashed the eggs in his beard and took the coffee and poured it over his head. When they were done harassing him, they walked away, laughing. The truck driver got up, paid the bill, and walked out. The bikers taunted him as he walked out, saying that he had no guts. About 10 minutes later, a guy walked into the diner and said, "Man, that truck driver really is a terrible driver! He just ran over three motorcycles out front!" Although our flesh likes the ending of this humorous story, forgiveness is about forgetting. God could run over those motorcycles if He wanted. Seriously, however, God's way is not about getting even. It's not talking about the person. It's letting go of our desire to strike back and choosing instead to let the Lord be in charge of vengeance.

As we continue reading in Judges, we find Samson saying, "One more time, and then I will stop." *"Samson said to them, 'Since you would do a thing like this, I will surely take revenge on you, and after that I will cease'"* (Judges 15:7). Does that sound like us? Just one more act of vengeance and then we won't do it anymore. As we read earlier, however, vengeance is never satisfied until we allow God to take control of it.

But Samson didn't stop. And it can be the same for us. We think to ourselves, *"I'm just going to lie this one time. I'm just going to flirt one more time. I'm just going to have one more drink. I'm just going to have one more slice of pizza. I'm just going to buy one more outfit."* Truly, out of the heart come the issues of life. If our heart and mind are focused on the Lord, we will think and behave according to God's Word. The fear of God will be in our heart. Yet if our heart and mind are focused on the lusts of the flesh, we will do whatever is necessary to fulfill those fleshly desires. Samson's heart was filled with every kind of lust. He refused to repent and turn from his sinfulness; therefore, the cycle of rebellion and revenge continued in his life.

The Spirit of God Came Upon Samson

"When he came to Lehi, the Philistines came shouting against him. Then the Spirit of the LORD came mightily upon

him; and the ropes that were on his arms became like flax that is burned with fire, and his bonds broke loose from his hands. He found a fresh jawbone of a donkey, reached out his hand and took it, and killed a thousand men with it" (Judges 15:14–15).

God wasn't done with Samson. It seems God would have had His fill of this fleshly man, but instead, the Spirit of God came upon him in spite of his sinful behavior. Similarly, God isn't done with us either. And that's so good to know! To understand God's endless grace and love toward us is both humbling and encouraging. What God has started in our life, He is also able to finish because He is committed to each one of us personally.

When I read the incredible story of Samson killing 1,000 enemy Philistines with the jawbone of a donkey, I am in awe of his strength. But I am also saddened to see the depth of sin Samson committed. I believe that God would have enabled Samson to take everybody out with his bare hands. Who put that jawbone of a donkey there? Was it the Holy Spirit, or was it Satan? Remember, Samson was not to touch anything that was dead. So clearly it wasn't the Holy Spirit telling him to reach down and defile himself. In addition, not only was it a dead animal; it was also an unclean animal. Samson knew that, but he didn't care. The Spirit of God came upon him, but he chose an unclean vessel as a weapon. He killed 1,000 men with it and afterward began to boast and make up a rhyme: *"With the jawbone of a donkey, heaps upon heaps, with the jawbone of a donkey I have slain a thousand men!"* (Judges 15:16).

When God anoints our life, we need to be very careful about what we touch. It is far better to trust God for our deliverance than for us to reach for that which is unclean. No matter what the world may say, the end does not justify the means. Samson was in total violation of God's law. He had no business at all hanging out with Philistine women. He had no business being in the vineyard. He had no business putting his hand in the dead lion and then making up a riddle about the way he had killed it. How dare he gloat over his sinful behavior in the vineyard with the lion and the honey! He should have been repenting and brokenhearted over it—not boasting about it. Finally, he had no business picking up the dead donkey's jawbone or making a rhyme that glorified his sinful behavior. Samson was clearly out of God's will, but even so, God used him to get His work done.

Amazingly, Samson then cried out to God, even while he had just repeatedly acted in sin: *"Then he became very thirsty; so he cried out to the LORD and said, 'You have given this great deliverance by the hand of Your servant; and now shall I die of thirst and fall into the hand of the uncircumcised?'"* (Judges 15:18).

Samson is basically crying out to God saying, "Don't You care about me?" Samson needed to learn a lesson. He boasted about what he did, so much so that he probably thought he was invincible. But immediately after his victory, he found himself in a crisis. In a sense, God was saying to Samson, "Pay attention! My power came upon you—that's why you had the victory. Now you're thirsty. You need to learn that you are weak without Me. You have needs in your life that only I can fulfill."

God Is Not Afraid to Show Us Ourselves

Many times after we have achieved great victories in our lives, we often experience deep lows as well. I believe the Lord allows these occurrences to remind us that we are human, we are weak, and without Him, we can do nothing. When Elijah experienced a great victory from God, immediately afterward he fell into a deep depression and wanted to commit suicide. (See 1 Kings 19:4.) Jeremiah was faithfully doing the work of God when he got beat up and put into stocks. He then cried out, "Lord, take my prophet badge; I'm out of here; I don't want to do this anymore; this is just too painful and hurtful." (See Jeremiah 20.) Even David, who enjoyed great success as king and military commander, was plagued by great personal hardship. He said, "Oh, how long, how long do I have to go through this? Your silence is killing me, and my rebellion has destroyed my time of worship." (See Psalm 51.)

What was God doing with Elijah, Jeremiah, and David? Why would He reveal their weaknesses to us? I believe He wants us to understand that He can do the very same thing for us in our generation as He did in each of their generations.

We need to remember that our God is the same in all generations—He never changes. He is the same yesterday, today, and tomorrow. God is not afraid to reveal our weaknesses. Sometimes, even to our own horror, He reveals our weaknesses to our family, friends, and even foes. Why? Because we are rebellious and not willing to listen—He wants us to turn to Him.

Poor Samson, what a mess he found himself in, all because he would not listen to and obey God. God wants to bless our lives and show Himself mighty on our behalf, just like He did for Samson. Yet just like Samson, the Lord allows difficulties to arise in our lives in order to drive us to our knees and reveal our helplessness and great need for God. Every once in a while, He will show us a need we can't fulfill. It might be a relationship we can't figure out or a situation we can't understand, but one thing we do know, we are helpless. These seemingly hopeless situations help us realize that God is the only One who can meet our needs and fill our hearts with peace. God is the One who can move mountains and do the impossible. We often need to be reminded that we are human and that God is the One who is supernaturally able.

God Clave a Hollow Place

"But God clave a hollow place that was in the jaw, and there came water thereout; and when he had drunk, his spirit came

again, and he revived: wherefore he called the name thereof Enhakkore, which is in Lehi unto this day" (Judges 15:19, KJV).

I love the way the Holy Spirit chose words and placed them in the Bible at just the right moment. In the King James Version, the word the Holy Spirit uses in Judges 15:19 is "but." This is the hinge that swings the doors of Scripture in such a powerful way. It's a word that either turns everything right side up or upside down. For example, Jacob said regarding Laban, "Yet your father has deceived me and changed my wages ten times, *but God* did not allow him to hurt me." (Gen 31:7). Luke said of Jesus, "*But God* raised him from the dead." (Acts 13:30). Finally, Paul the apostle said we were lost in our sins, *but God*, who is rich in mercy, saved us (Ephesians 2:4-5). "*But God*" helped Samson; always remember that "*But God*" helps you as well.

Points to Ponder:

- Am I willing to trust God even when circumstances don't seemingly go my way?

- Do I walk in forgiveness, or do I desire to get even?

- When my weaknesses are revealed, do I draw near to God, trust Him more, and know that He is able?

Chapter 5

DORMANT, BUT NOT DEAD

"Now Samson went to Gaza and saw a harlot there, and went in to her. When the Gazites were told, 'Samson has come here!' they surrounded the place and lay in wait for him all night at the gate of the city. They were quiet all night, saying, 'In the morning, when it is daylight, we will kill him.' And Samson lay low till midnight; then he arose at midnight, took hold of the doors of the gate of the city and the two gateposts, pulled them up, bar and all, put them on his shoulders, and carried them to the top of the hill that faces Hebron" (Judges 16:1–3).

Samson's Difficulty with God

From our perspective, it appears that God must have had a difficult time with Samson. Of course, we know that isn't true, but it seems so to us. I think we might want to believe that because sometimes we may wonder if God finds us difficult to deal with too. But we're not as complex as we'd like to believe we are, and neither was Samson.

No matter where we read in the Bible, God has never had difficulty with anyone or anything because He is omniscient. The word "omniscient" comes from the root word "omniscience"—which breaks down to omni, meaning "all," and science, meaning "knowledge"; God is all-knowing. And because He knows all things, nothing ever catches Him by surprise. He knows what all people, nations, and kingdoms are doing and why. God is also omnirighteous, which means He is all-righteous. His very nature is pure holiness, and all His ways and decisions are perfect, untainted by selfish ambitions. He's also omnipotent, meaning He's all-powerful. Nothing can turn Him nor challenge Him. He is the creator of all things. God Himself has said, *"Is there anything too hard for Me?"* (Jeremiah 32:27). Finally, God is also omnipresent, which means He is all-present. He fills His whole creation with His presence and glory. The writer of the book of Hebrews said that all things are open and naked to His eye. There's no place we can hide because He sees all things, and there's nowhere we can run that He's not already there. (Psalm 139).

So, because God is all-knowing, all-righteous, all-powerful, and all-present, we know that God couldn't have had a difficult time with Samson. God already knew ahead of time what Samson was going to say and do. He was not surprised by Samson's disobedience. Instead, it was Samson who had a difficult time with God.

Although he was called by God to serve, Samson was unwilling to yield what God demanded of him—the flesh. Samson had a lust problem, and the root cause of his lust was his selfish life, just as it is with us. Selfishness lives and breathes within every sin we will commit. Selfishness can dominate our whole life and reduce us down to one letter of the alphabet, "I." I am seeking to please myself. I am looking out for number one. I am going to get what I want, when I want it, and no one will be able to stop me. Doesn't that sound just like us when we are walking in our flesh? This self-centeredness eventually took Samson out of ministry and literally destroyed his life, as it can do to us as well.

Satan will never stop tempting us, and evil will never be very far.

Temptation Is Never Far Away

"Now Samson went to Gaza and saw a harlot there, and went in to her" (Judges 16:1).

Samson, once again, gives in to his lust and spends the night with a harlot. This is a reminder to us that although sin may become dormant, it never dies. It is also a reminder that sin will always be a problem in our lives until the day that God takes us home to Him. Until then, we will never be far from the presence of sin. Even though as believers we live a transformed life, Satan will never stop tempting us, and evil will never be very far. There will never be a moment or a day in which sin will not try to regain a foothold in our life. Satan will stir up our past habits and strive to bring us back into bondage once again. So let's not be fooled. Although God has redeemed and renewed our spirit, our fleshly bodies have not yet been redeemed. This is why we continue to pray not to be led into temptation and to be delivered from evil. We have to remain vigilant, and as we read about Samson, we see he was not.

An excellent example of past sin stirred up again is Moses, the great lawgiver. He had a problem with anger. Early in his life, he had killed an Egyptian man while in a rage. Consequently, he was driven into the desert because of what he had done, and guess who was waiting for him . . . none other than God. God had a work to do in Moses, and the desert was the perfect place to break his pride and his angry spirit. Those long years in the wilderness brought Moses' heart to the Lord, and then God prepared him to lead the people of Israel out of Egypt. However, toward the very end of Moses' life, his wicked anger exploded again; this time it was not toward an Egyptian, but rather toward God's own people.

The Bible tells us that God told Moses to speak to a specific rock and that water would flow from it for the children of Israel to drink (Numbers 20:8). But instead of speaking to the rock, Moses hit the rock—not once, but twice, out of anger—and it cost him the privilege of entering into the Promised Land. Moses had misrepresented God by hitting the rock, as if God were the one who was angry. But the Lord was not angry with the people—Moses was. So God then went to his servant Moses that day and spoke to his heart, telling him, "Moses, you can no longer lead My people. I love you, but you are disqualified." What a piercing reminder that sin will never cease to come after us.

Even so, if we accept His help, *"God is our refuge and strength, a very present help in trouble"* (Psalm 46:1). God had warned Cain in the Old Testament (Genesis 4) and told him, "Cain, it's not too late for you to love your brother, Abel. Turn from those evil thoughts about murdering your own brother." God warned Cain that sin was at his front door waiting to destroy his life and provided Himself as a refuge and strength from the evil in Cain's mind. But Cain, like Samson in later years, chose to be angry and rebellious. Cain refused to listen to God, and he killed his brother anyway. No one is safe from the power of sin. It never sleeps. It never dies, and it never misses an opportunity to ruin a life. Only God can provide us refuge from sin. He is our *"very present help in trouble"* (Psalm 46:1).

We face the same problem in our life. That one thing, whether it's pride, jealousy, insecurity, anger, lust, or greed, oftentimes becomes a battle that we fight for the rest of our life. Even though God may give us the victory (and there will be great moments), this thing will always try to return and destroy our witness, our ministry, and even our very life.

It is interesting to note that the times we are tempted the most are often after incredible victories. After King David prospered, he fell into sin. When Uzziah prospered for 51 years in the southern kingdom, he was then smitten with leprosy because he was prideful. He entered into the temple, choosing to violate the Word of god. (See 2 Chroncles 26:18-20). As I mentioned earlier in this book, when Elijah was doing a tremendous work for God, it was soon after that he wanted to commit suicide. We are not any different than these giants of faith. Just like them, we too have our moments of great victory. Our lives begin to prosper and things click into place, and then we fall because we take our eyes off of the Lord and begin to rely on our own abilities rather than God's abilities. Satan takes advantage of these times and tempts us when we feel invincible. Therefore, it's

> *Sin will never let us go. It's going to follow us.*

crucial we remember to *"lay aside every weight, and the sin which so easily ensnares us, and let us run with endurance the race that is set before us, looking unto Jesus, the author and finisher of our faith"* (Hebrews 12:1–2).

The Endurance of Sin

Sin will never let us go. It's going to follow us. It's going to wait for that right moment to slip into our life. We could have been married for 30 years and never been tempted to be unfaithful, until that one day when we are traveling away from our wife. When we left home, we had a fight with her and are still stewing over it. We go out to dinner with a client who decides to go to a popular bar in town. All of a sudden, an attractive woman is flirting with us and we are tempted to sin. If we yield, the sin will destroy us and the marriage. We need to remember that sin is out to destroy us. Whether it's today or 30 years down the road, sin will always seek to get believers to yield to its power. Remember, Samson's downfall was a result of his lifetime of yielding to sin in his life and refusing to yield to God's will. And Satan kept watch.

Without a doubt, Satan watched and waited for Samson. The end of Judges, chapter 15, tells us that Samson judged Israel for 20 years. He became a legal official and directed the Israelites in lawful matters. Still, after all this time, Samson returned to his old ways. What happened to Samson? What caused him to start lusting again? I believe he ran into some type of obstacle that challenged him. Oftentimes when we feel any type of pressure, we will run. Sometimes we run to the mall, other times we run to the refrigerator, and we may even run back to our old way of dealing with stress by drinking and/or taking drugs. If we have to run, we must run to God and let Him give us the grace to meet whatever need is overwhelming us.

So Samson went down again to the city of the Philistines. He was looking to once more satisfy his lust; he was returning to the place he should not have been. We can almost hear Satan whispering to him, "Samson, it's time to go where you are appreciated. You're so lonely. Look around Samson;

there's nothing to do in this town. Maybe God could use you over in the Philistine city again. You could show them the power of your God once again. They sure noticed you there before, and there are so many beautiful women there who will adore you."

Satan didn't lie to Samson; the Philistine city was a popular place to be, and the women were beautiful and plentiful. And it wasn't far. It was by the seaport of the Mediterranean, about three to four miles away. Sometimes Satan doesn't get to us with a lie; he'll tell the truth . . . but he doesn't tell us the consequences of that truth. For some reason, Samson loved the Philistine country, even though it was the place that always brought him destruction. Even so, he had forgotten about that in the excitement of what Satan was whispering to him. Samson was tempted and was caught once again.

More than anything else, I am fascinated that the temptation to sin will never, ever leave us. Sin and the devil will lie in wait like a roaring lion, and both will look for the right time to stumble us. Sin knows when we're lonely. It sees what we've been through, and it seeks to take us out by false comfort. We must turn to Christ. We can't deal with sin on our own. There is no reasoning with it. There are far too many people today who are trying to "slay the devil" and all sorts of nonsense. We need to understand that we alone cannot fight against the Enemy. Only Jesus Christ can go against Satan and win. We can't do it on our own merit. Even Michael, the archangel, wouldn't mess with Satan. He said, *"The Lord rebuke you!"* (Jude 9).

We cannot reason or "deal" with our sin. We need to be delivered. We need more of Jesus Christ in our life. Yet we would rather deal with our own sin than surrender our lives to Christ and let Him handle it. We would rather justify our attitude than ask God to change our heart. Our flesh does not want to yield. It refuses to humble itself, and that's why the Bible says, *"There is joy in the presence of the angels of God over one sinner who repents"* (Luke 15:10). When a person has lived a sinful life and then all of a sudden is finally willing to be obedient and walk before God, it is a joyous occasion. Turning from idols to serve the living God is a major event, not only in a person's life, but in heaven as well. That kind of change shows that God is working in a heart. It is the hope of glory. But make no mistake: It is God's glory, not our own. (See 1 Thessalonians 1:9).

The Excitement of Sin

Why is sin such a problem for us? Because it is exciting and fun! At least it appears to be in the beginning. Why eat broccoli when there's pizza? Why eat carrots when there are donuts? We love the quick fix, the immediate gratification, and the rebellion of sin. That's why fornication, adultery, drugs, and pornography thrive, because there is a sense of excitement and fun. If there were no enticement or promise of pleasure and satisfaction, we would not be tempted to sin. Let me tell you, when my wife says we are going to have a salad for dinner, I'm not excited. But when she says we are going to In and Out to get a burger, then I'm thrilled!

In our story, Samson is now lured to the city of the Philistines. But he doesn't want salad; he's going for the In and Out Burger. The city is an area that is filled with temptation for him—a thriving, exciting place with beautiful women. It is filled with sin. How often are we lured to places we shouldn't be? We think things like, *"I've heard there are a lot of new, interesting hotels on the Las Vegas strip. I think I will go check it out and get a cup of coffee at Starbucks."* We know we shouldn't go there, but we're hoping that God might open the doors for us anyway. However, God will never put us in a place that leads us to go against His Word.

Now Samson knew that he was not supposed to be with the Philistines, but he wanted to go down there and check it out, maybe meet some friends and definitely find another woman. But what Samson didn't realize was that by going down there, it was going to be the beginning of the end for him. This time, Samson will cross the line, and God will not bring him back. There are many times that we cross over the line, but God brings us back. There are many times we tempt the Lord, and God brings us back. And there are times when we get ourselves into bad situations, and God's redeeming love continues to bring us back. There will come a time, however, when the consequences of our actions catch up with us, and God will not rescue us out of them. This is what happened with Samson.

God Help Us

"There is a time we know not when, a line we know not where,
That marks the destiny of man, between sorrow and despair.
There is a line thou by man unseen. Once it has been crossed,
Even God and all His love has sworn, all is lost."

(Author Unknown)

Samson is about to reap some heavy consequences because he chose to go down to the Philistine city once again. Why did he go? Besides being lured by the sin, I think Samson thought he could whip the Philistines. Samson still felt he could get away with sinning and not have any repercussions. I believe that people who are in ministry often have an even greater temptation in this area. Because they are serving God, they mistakenly think that they can get away with a little sin and no one will ever know. Samson thought no one would ever know, and apparently he also pridefully thought that he could either talk or fight his way out of any trouble—but not this time.

So Samson went down to the Philistine city, and it just so happens (with God there are no coincidences) that there was a harlot waiting for him. That's interesting. But she was not just any harlot; she was a messenger from Satan himself. Without even batting an eye, Samson got excited and no doubt thought it was his lucky day. Why do we think that maybe God has opened the door for us when we are where we shouldn't be? We need to understand that Satan opens doors as well. We may think, *"Well, God opened the door for me to work here at this bar."* Really? God wants us to avoid the appearance of evil (see 1 Thessalonians 5:22, KJV). We think, *"Well, God opened the door for me to marry this nonbeliever."* Are we sure? God tells us not to be unequally yoked with an unbeliever (see 2 Corinthians 6:14). God is not going to open a door for us to go contrary to His will so that we might sin. He will never go against His own Word. It is not the Lord who tempts us; it is our flesh and Satan that tempt us to sin.

Samson loved to flirt with sin. He saw a prostitute and liked what he saw. Everything Samson saw, he wanted. Everything Samson wanted, he took. What a definition of selfishness. He was a man called by God, given the ability to minister and the authority to do whatever God wanted him to do, but he chose to use his God-given talent to satisfy his own flesh. Too often, we do the same. Satan will do things to get us excited about sin. He knows our weaknesses and tries to trip us up. Satan knows the sin that is dormant within us and fully desires to awaken it once again. We must be vigilant to not let Satan help us return to a sin from which we have been delivered. No matter what we may think, it won't satisfy us; it will only entrap us.

The Emptiness of Sin

Although sin is exciting for a season, it always leaves its victims unfulfilled. When we pursue a sinful life, a life fulfilling our fleshly desires, we end up feeling empty. Sadly, many people find themselves in a vicious cycle of trying to fill the void in their life with more pleasure and more sin. It never works; it just leaves them feeling more miserable, more alone, and emptier than ever before. So, why did Samson go back to the Philistine city? Why did he go after a harlot? Was there something missing in his life? Although we'll never know for sure about Samson, we do need to ask ourselves the same questions: Why do I have to go out? Why do I have to have a date? Why do I have to get out of this marriage? Why do I have to get another job? Why do I have to have another car? We still have the opportunity to examine ourselves, listen to God, and sidestep the roaring lion.

Satan will do things to get us excited about sin.

I remember the time I bought a new Jeep Wrangler. I was so excited. I took my wife up to the mountains, and we bounced all over the place. The ride was so rough because the wheelbase was too short. We both had a tremendous headache and neckache from the bouncy ride. But I liked it anyway, and I wanted it. After all, it was my money. Of course, my wife promptly reminded me it wasn't actually mine, but rather, it was God's money. The whole trip to the mountain, however, made me think about why I bought the jeep, and that turned out to be the million dollar question. In fact, I knew the answer before even asking the question. I bought the jeep because I thought it would make me happy. What a horrible reason to buy anything.

We buy things to make us happy, don't we? What we need to understand is that our home, our car, our kids, or our job will never satisfy the void in our heart. Neither will seeking after our own pleasure satisfy the emptiness inside us. Only one thing will fulfill us. Only one thing will give us the inner peace that we are longing for—and that is the peace of God. When we have an intimate relationship with God, we will have the peace of God in our heart. First we have peace with God. All our sins are forgiven and have been dealt with by His cross. We are forgiven and are reconciled. Second, we have the peace of God. We are not worried about anything nor is there anxiety. We trust. And finally, we have peace from God. Now we can share Christ and with confidence and not worry about what people think.

Samson, however, went down to the Philistine city looking. He went down searching. He went down hoping to satisfy his flesh. He wanted something to fill the void in his life. But sin will always leave us empty. Jesus said to the woman at the well, "Whoever drinks of this water will thirst again" (John 4:13). He knew that she was searching. She had been through five husbands yet couldn't find contentment. Jesus knew what she really needed. Are you searching and trying to fill the void? Have you discovered that sin leaves you nothing but empty? Turn to the Lord. Only He can satisfy you.

The Evil of Sin

"When the Gazites were told, 'Samson has come here!' they surrounded the place and lay in wait for him all night at the gate of the city. They were quiet all night, saying, 'In the morning, when it is daylight, we will kill him'" (Judges 16:2).

The enemy knew that Samson was in town and whom he was with. In fact, they were now beginning to set him up to ambush him. Make no mistake, however fun sin may be, it is evil. Its end goal is to destroy our life. Samson should never have been there in the first place, but because he was, the Philistines were going to make sure he would reap the consequences.

Remember the story of Joseph and Potiphar's wife (Genesis 39)? Joseph is praised, and rightly so, for his response to his master's wife's advances. He ran! But in thinking about the situation, we see that Joseph actually gave the Enemy opportunity. What was he doing alone in the house with another man's wife? He knew his master was away. He could have had others with him to protect him from one of the most subtle sins of all—the appearance of evil. Joseph should never have been there.

We must avoid the appearance of evil and flee temptation rather than giving it an opportunity in our lives. Why put ourselves in a difficult situation? Why expose ourselves to a great temptation? I have heard over and over throughout my years in ministry how singles have fallen into sin. It's seldom out in public; rather, it's just the opposite. Two people are by themselves, and guess what? They planned it that way, and they were hoping it all would work in their favor. They have created the moment or mood. They have this special person over for dinner, just the two of them. The house is empty, friends are all gone, music is playing, lights are dimmed, and candles are flickering—now what? After this great dinner, what do they do? They take it to the next level. Now they have become an instrument of Satan himself.

Young people, be extremely careful not to be caught like Samson, going places you should not go and making excuses for what should not have happened. It's not that we do not trust you. You should not trust yourselves. Your flesh is just too strong to stop. So I say, if you cannot stop it, you should not start it. Don't set yourself up for an ambush like Samson did.

Sin is evil, but it's also very subtle and cunning. It will tell us that it is okay to flirt a little. So what if we are married? There's no harm in a little flirting. And sin will tell us that it's okay to smoke that one joint. After all, it's just one. What harm can come from smoking one joint? Or sin will tell us, it's just a little white lie. Everyone lies a little bit. But sin never, ever, tells us the consequences. It doesn't tell us that we can lose our family, lose our kids, lose our business, or lose our very life. Satan won't tell us that. Satan entices us using our own weaknesses, gets us to yield, and then lowers the boom.

So Samson's enemies are now lying in ambush for him. They lock the gates to the city so that he has no way out. Here we see that ultimately, sin will lock the door so that we are in bondage to it and have no way out. All of a sudden, we find that we are addicted to pornography. All of a sudden,

> *But sin never, ever, tells us the consequences.*

we find we are a drug addict or an alcoholic. All of a sudden, we find that we are divorced, our kids hate us, and the woman we had the affair with is long gone. And we think, *"What happened? How did I get here?"* We followed the lure of sin and allowed it to grow and dominate our life. Now we are in bondage to the very sin that seemed so pleasing in the beginning.

Samson's Strength

"And Samson lay low till midnight; then he arose at midnight, took hold of the doors of the gate of the city and the two gateposts, pulled them up, bar and all, put them on his shoulders, and carried them to the top of the hill that faces Hebron" (Judges 16:3).

Just how strong was Samson? Consider what Judges 16:3 states. It is believed that the gates of the city were anywhere from 30 to 40 feet wide and from 20 to 30 feet high. They could easily have weighed an incredible two tons. He carried these huge gates and poles 20–30 miles up the hill that faces Hebron. It was an amazing feat.

We can just picture Samson doing this to mock the Philistines, can't we? Even though he had a tremendous gift, he was a foolish man in that he used his amazing strength for his own gain and to show off. God gave Samson the ability to have great physical strength, but Samson never acknowledged that his strength came from God. Sadder yet, he really didn't want to understand it.

God so often takes someone who is weak and makes them strong. Why? He does that so the glory goes to the Lord alone and not to another human being. Only God can make weak people strong. But even though the Lord gave Samson his strength, Samson took the credit for his own glory. Yes, men feared him (and he must have enjoyed that!), but the real problem was that he didn't fear God.

Samson had power without humility. Humility is borne out of power. If God in His grace has given me His authority, it should humble me and break me. If God is using me, I should really be baffled, not prideful. Nehemiah said to the people, "We did not eat of the king's table, nor did we take of their money." (See Nehemiah 5: 17-18). In other words, we could have done this, but we didn't want to abuse our authority—we wanted to set an example. Nehemiah possessed humility. God gives us the power, position, or talent to help people and to minister to them, not to embarrass or manipulate them and certainly not to use them for our own glory.

The End of Sin

Samson did not fear God. I find it interesting that he could destroy a lion but he couldn't surrender his pride. He could break the bands of the ropes that bound him, but he couldn't listen to the Holy Spirit. Even though he had great physical strength, he was so weak in the realm of the spirit that his life was marred and destroyed. Proverbs 16:18 exhorts, *"Pride goes before destruction, and a haughty spirit before a fall."* Now, we are going to see a man whom God chose, a man whom God blessed, and a man whom God empowered lose his ministry, his freedom, his eyes, and his very life—because he was filled with pride and refused to surrender to and obey the Lord.

The end of sin is destruction. Samson toyed with it, flirted with it, and then became enslaved to it. Now sin was going to have its say in Samson's life and will eventually destroy him. God help us to heed the Spirit's warning when we are going off track and turn back to our gracious Father before sin destroys us.

Points to Ponder:

- Are there any areas of past sin in my life that are easily stirred? Where do I need to continually guard myself with the full armor of God?

- Is there anything in my life that I think I am "getting away with"?

- Do I truly fear God?

Chapter 6

THE ART OF SEDUCTION

"Afterward it happened that he loved a woman in the Valley of Sorek, whose name was Delilah. And the lords of the Philistines came up to her and said to her, 'Entice him, and find out where his great strength lies, and by what means we may overpower him, that we may bind him to afflict him; and every one of us will give you eleven hundred pieces of silver'" (Judges 16:4–5).

Lust Untamed

Samson's lust was out of control. It was the very thing that had caused him to waste away his life, and now it was about to completely destroy him. His lust had started as a small flickering flame that eventually exploded into a forest fire. It became master over his very being, possessing every thought and passion of his life. All Samson could think about was himself and how to satisfy his own fleshly desires. He was no longer concerned about God's will or His people. Even worse, Samson was no longer concerned about the enemy. Lust never starts off that way; it begins as only a thought, but unchecked it can turn into a horrific beast, consuming our whole life. Lust will destroy a marriage; it will cheat children out of time with their parents; it will ruin a person's witness at work; and it will sear a conscience and produce an emotional wreck.

Lust Ruling

Lust ruled all of the relationships Samson had with women. The Bible only tells us of three, but it's a good guess there were more. He had the relationship in Timnah, where he wanted to marry one of the Philistine women. Then later he spent time and was intimate with a harlot in Gaza. Last, he became involved with a woman named Delilah. Through His mercy and forgiveness, God delivered Samson from the consequences of the first two bad relationships. But

> *Samson did what we all too often do—he mistook God's grace for His approval.*

unfortunately, Samson did what we all too often do—he mistook God's grace for His approval. As a result, Samson's pride and sin deceived him into thinking he could get away with just about anything.

I think there are times in our lives when we honestly believe that we are getting away with sin. On the contrary, we are misunderstanding God's mercy and righteousness. God isn't letting us get away with anything. Rather, He is graciously allowing us time to repent. The Lord desires that we turn away from sin immediately, but He will give us a season of time to learn the importance of a life of repentance. We need to understand that just because God doesn't judge or deal with our sin immediately, it does not mean that He is approving our actions. When we believe that we are getting away with sin, we give birth to the idea that we are not only above other people, but above the Word of God as well. Samson felt that he was above his parents, above his friends, and ultimately, above his Lord. God had no other choice but to lay him low; it was a devastating blow.

Lust Seeking

We pick up the story in Judges 16:4, which explains that Samson was in the Valley of Sorek and that he was in love with a woman named Delilah. Sorek is a word that means grapes. Remember, according to the Nazirite vow, Samson was not to be around grapes nor was he to be in the Philistine town. But once again, Samson was in a place he should not have been and with a woman who should have been off limits to him. Sorek was a border town to Israel, just like Tijuana, Mexico, is a border town to San Diego, California. A border town is much like a Christian straddling the fence between the flesh and the spirit. We are tempted to cross over and have a good time; however, the reality is that we need to get away from those areas of our lives that are dangerous. Often, our mentality is that we can jump across, live in sin, and then come back. But, boy, being caught and thrown in a Tijuana jail will be the opposite of a fun time.

Lust Satisfied

Samson was crossing over into the border town, and Delilah was the bridge—a bridge that brought Samson into the Philistine world. Sadly, she was also a bridge that was going to destroy the work of God in his life. The five Philistine kings were each willing to give 1,100 pieces of silver (5,500 in total) to Delilah for enticing Samson and uncovering the secret of his strength. To become an overnight millionaire, all she had to do was seduce Samson and turn him over to the Philistines. Judges 16:6 reads, *"So Delilah said to Samson, 'Please tell me where your great strength lies, and with what you may be bound to afflict you.'"*

The truth is that lust is never satisfied. The flesh is unquenchable. The Word tells us, however, *"In Your [the Lord's] presence is fullness of joy; at Your right hand are pleasures forevermore"* (Psalm 16:11). *And only "He satisfies the longing soul, and fills the hungry soul with goodness"* (Psalm 107:9). True, lasting satisfaction can only be found in the Lord.

Lust Pleading

I can almost hear Delilah say, "Hey, Samson, sweetheart, tell me your secret so I can personally destroy you. Tell me everything I need to know to annihilate you and take away everything good in your life." And Samson, lying in her arms, blindly in love with her, just took it all in as if it were a seductive game. I'm sure Delilah's beauty blinded Samson from seeing that Satan had scripted the whole scene. Satan knew Samson's weaknesses: women and his pride. Delilah was enticing and offering pleasure, and Samson thought himself to be invincible. What a deadly combination. Four times she entrapped Samson, literally using him for her personal gain. She allowed the leaders of her city to lie in wait for him to reveal the source of his strength. Three times, Samson lied to her. Not only did he make her look foolish with the Philistines, but he was also communicating to her that maybe he did not really love her. Although Samson challenged Delilah's feminine arts, she turned up the heat and got her way in the end.

It is legitimate to think, *"Samson was an idiot. Couldn't he see what she was doing?"* I agree. But how often do we get ourselves into similar situations that can cause our lives such great destruction? We become starry-eyed and say things like, "But she's so cute" or "He's such a great guy." Sin blinds, and when people are living sinful, destructive lives, they don't want to hear the truth. They don't want counsel or correction. They are focused on satisfying their own desires, not on the wisdom God has provided us in His Word.

How often do we try to tell our teenagers that what they are doing is wrong, but they don't want to hear it? How often do we try to help a friend whom we see going down a wrong path, but he or she doesn't want our honesty? In other words, these people are hooked where they want to be hooked, and they don't want to hear the truth. Going down the road of sin will blind us. Remember, Satan wants to steal, kill, and destroy. He will make our life worthless and see to it that we have no testimony for Christ. Satan will begin to set traps that we know will destroy us, but we really don't want to see that truth.

Lust Persuading

"For the lips of an immoral woman drip honey, and her mouth is smoother than oil; but in the end she is bitter as wormwood, sharp as a two-edged sword. Her feet go down to death, her steps lay hold of hell" (Proverbs 5:3–5).

At first, Delilah came on to Samson with kind words— she was seductive and enticing. But once she had his attention, her words became bitter. Once she knew that she had him hooked, she played to his pride and to his ego. We should consider the wisdom in Proverbs 7:21–23: *"With her enticing speech she caused him to yield, with her flattering lips she seduced him. Immediately he went after her, as an ox goes to the slaughter, or as a fool to the correction of the stocks, till an arrow struck his liver. As a bird hastens to the snare, he did not know it would cost his life."*

It's amazing how persuasive a woman can be toward a man. Fortunately for me, my wife is a godly woman. One day, she asked me if I would paint one of the bathrooms in our house. Then when I was finished, there was half of a gallon of paint left over and she asked me about the bathroom upstairs. Well, when all was said and done, I had painted two bathrooms and a bedroom. Instead of just one bathroom, my wife got three rooms painted. How does she do that?

Delilah lured Samson and appealed to his lust. She used her power of seduction and cunning to influence and trap Samson with his own weakness. Because she knew his weakness, she was able to deceive him and destroy him. Hiding our weakness or leaving lust unchecked in our heart will always lead to destruction, just as it did with Samson.

Guarding the Heart

"And it came to pass, when she pestered him daily with her words and pressed him, so that his soul was vexed to death, that he told her all his heart, and said to her, 'No razor has ever come upon my head, for I have been a Nazirite to God from my mother's womb. If I am shaven, then my strength will leave me, and I shall become weak, and be like any other man'" (Judges 16:16–17).

The pressure was on, and Samson was breaking. We know we are breaking when we start giving in to our weakness. We know we are in trouble when we are now sipping that alcoholic drink or once again doing the things that we know we shouldn't do.

This woman got to Samson—like a bullet shattering glass or like a silent arrow striking its target. She was like a dripping faucet that drove him crazy. But she used the art of seduction and appealed to his physical prowess. Because of this, Samson finally shared all of his heart with Delilah. The key to his downfall was that Samson went too far and shared his heart with a woman who would ultimately destroy him. Jesus said, *"Where your treasure is, there your heart will be also"* (Matthew 6:21).

It is dangerous to open our heart to the wrong person. In the Old Testament, King Hezekiah was feeling pretty good one day. It seemed that the land was at peace and all was right with the world at that moment. It was then that he opened the treasure house to messengers from the king of Babylon. When the king realized everything that Hezekiah had, especially all the gold, he vowed to himself to make a plan and come back and take it (2 Kings 20:12–13).

...adultery rarely starts as a purely sexual thing, but rather as a friendship and with a sharing of thoughts

Too often in dating relationships, people open their hearts too quickly, and then they get hurt. It is also interesting to note that adultery rarely starts as a purely sexual thing, but rather as a friendship and with a sharing of thoughts. A relationship that begins this way often leads to people opening their hearts to one another and then finding themselves involved sexually as well.

For example, when it comes to believers, it would be like a brother in the faith saying to another gal, "Hey, how are you doing?" And after she tells him what God is doing in her life, she shares with him a special verse. He in turn shares a verse with her. Unsuspectingly, he begins to pour his devotional life into this Christian sister rather than with his spouse. Now there is a spiritual connection—whether he knows it or not, he has basically given his heart to this woman, and the fleshly connection is just right around the corner.

We need to be very careful about opening our heart in a dating relationship or in any friendship. God knows our heart, and our spouse needs to know our heart, but no one else needs to know it. Even when sharing our problems with friends or asking for prayer, I believe we need to be careful with whom we share these things. Our heart is a valuable treasure; we must guard it well.

Samson finally blew it big time by sharing his heart with this wicked woman. He had been flirting with all the promises of God; he had been hanging out in the vineyard; and he had been touching things that were dead. In fact, Samson had broken every vow of being a Nazirite except one—shaving his head. Then, when he revealed his secret to Delilah, even that vow was broken. We need to understand that Samson's strength was not in his long hair. People often think that his strength was in his hair, but his strength was really in keeping his commitment to God. However, because he told Delilah his secret, Samson's commitment was broken, his anointing removed, and the Philistines would surely shave his head.

"When Delilah saw that he had told her all his heart, she sent and called for the lords of the Philistines, saying, 'Come up once more, for he has told me all his heart.' So the lords of the Philistines came up to her and brought the money in their hand" (Judges 16:18).

This story reminds me of Judas betraying Jesus for 30 pieces of silver. Judas was a man who could be bought, just like these kings bought Delilah. Here was a woman who supposedly loved Samson—a woman he had been enamored with—nagging him day and night to find out the secret of his strength just so she could turn him over to the enemy and get paid for doing so. Samson was so blinded by his sin that he didn't even recognize he had opened his heart to the enemy.

Sin Blinds Us

"Then she lulled him to sleep on her knees, and called for a man and had him shave off the seven locks of his head. Then she began to torment him, and his strength left him. And she said, 'The Philistines are upon you, Samson!' So he awoke from his sleep, and said, 'I will go out as before, at other times, and shake myself free!' But he did not know that the LORD had departed from him" (Judges 16:19–20).

Crossing the Line

Samson woke up thinking he would leave her home as he had done before; he believed in his own strength. He thought to himself, *"Hey, I've done it before and will do it again."* Samson really believed that he could deliver himself because, after all, he had previously done so on many occasions—remember the gates, the Philistines, the foxes, and so on. In fact, I am convinced that Samson believed he could still get out of the mess he was in, even though they had cut his hair. He thought, *"Hey, go ahead and cut my hair; nothing is going to happen to me."* That is why he finally told Delilah the truth.

Samson's selfishness pushed God too far—he crossed over the line and challenged God's grace and mercy for the last time. He was acting as though he was God, believing nothing could get in his way. Sadly, Samson was about to lose everything. His foolish selfishness and self-centeredness caused him to ruin his relationship with God. Samson never saw God's grace. Instead of relying on the Lord, he relied on himself. His commitment to the Lord was continually broken, and he barely recognized God in his life. That is why he didn't even realize that the Lord had departed from him. What a tragic situation.

I believe the only hope that we have in the battle against sin and against the Enemy is to cry out with all our heart, "God, have mercy upon me. Send Your Holy Spirit and deliver me!" Unfortunately, in our own minds, we feel we can get away with sin and sidestep the consequences. But there will come a time when God will say, "You mocked Me." The Scriptures are clear: "Whatever a man sows, that he will also reap" (Galatians 6:7).

I wonder what was going through Samson's mind as the Philistines grabbed him and he could neither move them nor throw them aside. He simply was overtaken by them—they bound him, plucked out his eyes, and took him away. He had lost his power and his anointing. What a horrible wake-up call!

Sometimes we think something is only a one-time thing, but it oftentimes becomes a lifetime issue. Samson was always in the wrong country, with the wrong women. He chased after ungodly women and had a one-night stand with a harlot. I think this fact is important. We might think, "I am just going to take this heroin one time," but then it has us. Or we think, *"I am just going to get involved in this one extramarital affair,"* and then we're hooked. *"I am going to click on that link one time on the Internet,"* and then the pornography has trapped us. "I am just going to gamble this one last time," and now our life savings are gone. *"I am just going to go window-shopping in the mall,"* and hours later, our VISA card is tapped out. *"I am just going to eat this one little piece of pie,"* but it tastes so good that we treat ourselves to a few more pieces until we've consumed the whole pie. The Bible is clear that sin never stops—it just gets worse and worse. It starts off with just one small thing and eventually controls everything in our life. Samson might have thought to himself: *"It's just a one-night stand; what's the problem? I am not hurting anyone."* Sin will always say, "It's just once in a while, and it's worth it."

We need to wake up. Sin is no less putrid or horrible if we only partake once in a while. Samson never took his commitment to the Lord seriously; too often he laughed at and mocked God's commandments. Sin was something that was fun to him, something he could do once in a while and not get burned.

Why couldn't Samson see the danger of being with Delilah? The answer is because he was simply blinded by all the sin in his life. That's what sin does: It blinds us to reality and to the things of God; it puts us in a place in which we think that we are above everything else; it leads us to the point at which we are not making good decisions. And before we know it, we are living with the enemy. We are living on the wrong side of the fence with no fear of God in our heart whatsoever. That is the power of sin.

> *We need to wake up. Sin is no less putrid or horrible if we only partake once in a while.*

The major problem in Samson's life was his prideful attitude and wrong line of thinking: *"I am smarter than God. God is not going to deal with me because I am in charge. I am smarter than my mom and dad. No one is going to tell me what to do or whom to marry. I want that woman—get her for me. I can fight my way out of anything. Nothing can touch me."*

But God made it clear that this final incident was the end of the line for Samson—he gambled with sin too many times and was now going to have to pay the consequences. The Lord had given him a ministry, immense power, and everything he could ever want. But every time God wanted him to do something for Israel, Samson was over in the Philistine town, lusting, acting greedy, showing off, and mocking people with the strength that God had given him. Samson crossed the line and was now finished.

How the Enemy Distracts Us from God

Satan seeks to send things into our life that will distract us from God. It is important to know that Delilah was a woman on a mission—a mission from hell. The kings of the Philistines were paying her, and Satan himself put them up to it. Just as Samson had a purpose, Delilah also had a calling—given to her by the Enemy—to destroy Samson. She was a woman's nightmare and a man's delight. Delilah was incredibly corrupt, and she knew how to entangle Samson. She was tenacious; she kept on going after him until she accomplished her mission. This woman went after the prophet of God, and she destroyed him.

Satan is going to seek to do everything he can in our life to bring us down. Our "Delilah" doesn't need to be a woman—it can be a job, a hobby, or even charitable activities and seemingly good works. It can be anything within our life that takes us away from the true calling of God. Satan will use people, circumstances, obstacles, and possessions to distract us from the call of God upon our lives. It takes great commitment to stay faithful. But Samson lacked the commitment to God that he needed to stay focused and get the job done without being distracted by the Enemy's lures. As a result, he got caught in Satan's traps and wasted his God-given power and potential.

God Still Loved Samson

When all was said and done, God still loved Samson. In a sense, the Lord was saying to Samson, "I will always love you, but you were never the instrument I wanted. I used you in spite of who you were. I saved you from that lion. I saved you in that vineyard. I saved you from the Philistines. I saved you from that woman in Timnah. I saved you from that harlot. But you have to learn a lesson, Samson: There are going to be consequences for your actions. Even so, I forgive you and I still love you." It is this love that never let go of Samson; in the same way, God's love will never let go of us.

God gave Samson one more chance, and he finally passed the test. But he lost his life in the process. May God help us learn a vital lesson in our lives: When we sin and think we have gotten away with something, we must pray for God to send His Holy Spirit and remind us that it's time to repent. May we all repent and turn from our sin before

God has to deal with our foolishness. We don't want to waste our gifts and talents as Samson did. The consequences are too costly, the pain too horrific.

Points to Ponder:

- Do I desire truth, and am I open to counsel and correction?

- Do I guard my heart?

- Am I serious about my commitment to the Lord? Do I love His Word and desire to walk in His commandments?

Chapter 7

THE RESTORATION OF A FAILURE

"Now the temple was full of men and women. All the lords of the Philistines were there—about three thousand men and women on the roof watching while Samson performed. Then Samson called to the LORD, saying, 'O Lord God, remember me, I pray! Strengthen me, I pray, just this once, O God, that I may with one blow take vengeance on the Philistines for my two eyes!' And Samson took hold of the two middle pillars which supported the temple, and he braced himself against them, one on his right and the other on his left. Then Samson said, 'Let me die with the Philistines!' And he pushed with all his might, and the temple fell on the lords and all the people who were in it. So the dead that he killed at his death were more than he had killed in his life" (Judges 16:27–30).

The book of Hebrews contains one of the great chapters of the Bible—chapter 11. It's about faith, and it has been given many nicknames: The Heroes of Faith, The Honor Roll of the Old Testament Saints, The Hall of Faith, The Triumph of Faith, and simply, The Faith Chapter. Faith means believing in things not seen and trusting God to intervene in our life. I have heard it put this way: You may not know what the future holds, but you know who holds the future. Those listed in this special chapter on faith had responded to God in obedience, regardless of the consequences, and had been willing to let God move in their lives as He saw fit. Although Samson, for the most part, wasted his life and rebelled against God's Word, he still was mentioned in this Hall of Faith.

Hebrews 11:32 reads, *"And what more shall I say? For the time would fail me to tell of Gideon and Barak and Samson and Jephthah, also of David and Samuel and the prophets."* Why did the author of Hebrews list Samson in this Hall of Faith? I believe the greatest reason Samson is listed in Hebrews 11 is because he was ultimately willing to allow God to change him. Even though it was in the last few minutes of his life, Samson was willing to turn back to God despite his lifetime of failures. God's grace and forgiveness here really are amazing; if only Samson had embraced them sooner, he could have avoided so many horrible consequences.

The Humble and Obedient Life

A very sad commentary on our lives is that some just give up. Maybe we feel like we are never going to be able to change, so we just walk away from our faith or perhaps settle for a substandard Christian life. If we can learn anything from the life of Samson, it's that anybody can change at any time. Even though our life hasn't worked out as we would have liked and we have made some bad decisions, God can still restore us. Just as with Samson, it is never too late for God to do a powerful work in a person's life. Samson was finally broken before God when he decided not to turn away from Him but instead to humble himself and to allow God's will.

Wouldn't we think that when people are dealt with by God, they would humble themselves and surrender to the Lord? Unfortunately, many times, that is not the case. In fact, more often I have found just the opposite—people blame God instead of accepting responsibility for their own sinfulness. Have you ever tried to correct someone in love? What is their response? Have you ever shared with your children how they might be making a mistake in their life? Too often, their reaction is not one of humility, but of anger and rebellion. Instead of embracing your loving correction, they fight against you and reject altogether what you have to say . . . they just don't want to hear it.

people blame God instead of accepting responsibility for their own sinfulness.

Obedience, despite what we may think of it, is in actuality the greatest blessing of our life. Obedience means words or actions in compliance with *rightful* authority. Our sinful nature doesn't like obedience; its inclination is to fight authority. But the key here is compliance to a rightful authority. Any obedience the Lord requires from us is right and for our blessing. It is never too late to turn to God. Whether we have made a wrong decision in our marriage, gotten a divorce, become separated from our spouse, or if we are struggling with habitual sin, pornography, or even adultery, it is never too late to allow God to change us. If we can turn and look to God, repent, and accept His way in obedience, then we, too, will be given a place in the Hall of Faith.

Throughout Samson's life, he was not obedient, so God dealt severely with him. God allowed Samson's head to be shaved and his eyes to be gouged out. God allowed him to be bound in prison, beaten, and mocked by the enemy. Finally, after 20 years of living life on his own terms and being disobedient before the Lord, Samson let go and surrendered to God. It was the beginning of Samson's restoration when he cried out to the Lord, "God, strengthen me one more time and let me die with the Philistines." To which God answered, "Fine, let's do this thing." So God restored Samson's strength, and Samson ended up killing more enemies in just a few minutes than he had in his entire lifetime; his final obedience saved him: "So the dead that he killed at his death were more than he had killed in his life" (Judges 16:30).

The Way of the Transgressor Is Hard

At the end of his life, Samson found himself in a devastating situation. He had sinned against God with abandon throughout his life, but now it had all caught up to him; God was dealing with his rebellion. Samson was in a Philistine prison when he finally came to the end of himself and realized the error of his ways. This was a horrible place in which to be—especially when it didn't have to end like this. I'm reminded of the story of the prodigal son in Luke 15. He was the younger son of a rich man. This son had asked for his inheritance early, only to then waste all of the money on drinking and loose living until he eventually found himself feeding pigs and eating their slop to keep from starving. The Scripture reads that he stopped and *came to himself.* He saw the error of his ways and realized that the lowest servant on his father's estate still lived better than he was living. He turned from his ways and returned home to his father to beg to be taken in as a servant.

However, when the father saw his son coming down the road toward home, he ran to his son, put the family ring on his finger, and threw a party to celebrate because his son, who was once dead, was now alive again. The father refused to take him as a servant because he believed once a son, always a son. Living the life of a transgressor is hard, but God's ways are perfect and restoring to the soul. Although it took Samson a lifetime to come to himself, nonetheless, he acted in a similar way to the prodigal son when he finally stopped fighting against God. Samson asked God to strengthen him one last time. He knew that it was the end of his life, and he finally wanted to get it right.

Samson's Sin Took Him Further than He Wanted to Go

One sin can snowball into many, allowing Satan to entangle us in lifestyles that are far from God's will and purpose for our life. Samson went to Gaza (a place where he should not have gone), met up with a harlot (a woman he should not have been with), fell in love with Delilah (an unequally yoked relationship), and opened his heart to the enemy. One sin led to another and snowballed into his final destruction. Sin blinds us to the will of God. When we don't repent of our sin immediately, we give Satan room to continue to entice us and take us further down a road that leads to bondage and a broken fellowship with God. Lust is never satisfied; it's progressive. What used to stir us before is no longer enough to fulfill our desire today; lust needs to be fed more and more so that it can satisfy our own growing appetite for it. It becomes a slippery slope, and it's hard to keep from sliding down it. Sin will always take us further than we had ever intended to go.

Samson's Sin Kept Him Longer than He Wanted to Stay

Samson should never have been at Delilah's house, but once he went there, he ended up staying too long. The longer Samson stayed with her, the more she pressed him, and the more she challenged him. Delilah vexed Samson's soul to the point of death. He knew she was up to no good the first time she tried to entrap him, but instead of running away from her, he continued to linger at her home. He stayed despite the impending danger that should have caused him to flee, possibly because the excitement of the forbidden Delilah was too intoxicating for Samson to resist. Possibly he stayed because of his arrogance and confidence in his own ability to save himself as he had always done in the past. But ultimately, it was sin that kept Samson where he shouldn't have been, and it was sin that led to his destruction.

Samson is an example of what not to do. Joseph, on the other hand, gives us a picture of victory. We mentioned Joseph in Potiphar's house back in chapter 5. Potiphar's wife made advances upon Joseph several times, and he continually refused her. But it happened one day that he was in a place he should not have been: alone in the home of his master, with his master's wife. However, victory reigns in Joseph's life because he ran. Joseph fled from Potiphar's wife and ran outside (Genesis 39:12). Do not let sin, or the temptation to sin, keep you—instead, run!

Samson's Sin Cost Him More Than He Wanted to Pay

Samson paid for his sin with his freedom, his reputation, his testimony, and finally his life. Sin always costs more than what we intended to pay. It starts with a simple flirt, an innocent lunch, or a peck on the cheek. But now there's a pregnancy, a divorce, and our whole life is a mess. Sin has taken us further, and cost us more, than we ever expected.

Jesus Christ came to die for our sins because He understood what sin does to humanity: Sin destroys humanity. That is why the Holy Spirit doesn't want us to fool around with sin; He wants us to die spiritually to ourselves and to our sins. Jesus hung on the cross so that we do not have to be destroyed by sin.

God Released Him

Samson had never known defeat in his life. He had always been physically victorious, and nothing had ever happened in his life to challenge that. If he wanted to catch a fox, he could, with no problem—even 300 of them. And no one had ever been able to take away his strength—until Delilah. However, we need to realize that it wasn't because Delilah was so special that Samson lost his strength; he lost his strength because God had left him. When God removed His presence, Samson became just a normal man—there was no longer a supernatural strength. Once the covenant was violated, Samson was finished. He had played with God, had challenged God, and had even mocked God. Finally, the Lord said, "You have crossed over the line. You have sinned to the point that I'm going to take My hand of protection from you, and now you have to deal with the consequences of your sin."

The worst day we could ever experience would be if the Spirit of God departed from us. Can we imagine the Rapture coming, and all of a sudden our family is gone but we're still here? Can we imagine walking down the street and, suddenly, everyone is gone but us? Can we even begin to comprehend that, because of the lifestyle we have led and our unbelief, God has left us behind? We have played with God's kindness and gambled on our ability to convince Him that we are right with Him, but when He called us, our heart was empty, and we were left behind. Seriously, do we really think we can outsmart God?

The worst moment we could ever experience would be for God to remove His presence from us and allow the Enemy to come against us. The Old Testament speaks of how God raised adversaries to come against Solomon. In 1 Kings 11, several different adversaries came against Solomon because he was out of God's will and refused to listen to God's instruction. Adversaries can be anything from actual enemies to the loss of a job or marriage—anything that will change our focus and cause us to turn our back to the One who truly loves us.

Finally, the Lord said, "You have crossed over the line.

God sometimes allows adversaries to come upon His people because they are not sincere about following Him; they just don't take their commitment to Him seriously. And although God has great patience and mercy, He also has limits. When we continue to rebel and reject the Lord's will, a time will come when God simply says, "You have crossed the line. Let all the things that you've placed above Me—your false loves, your idolatry—take over your life."

Billy Graham once said, "If God doesn't judge the United States, He owes Sodom and Gomorrah an apology." Our country is filled with immorality and rebellion against God. I believe that the only reason God hasn't judged the United States is because we have not yet turned against the nation of Israel. In my opinion, if we ever turn on Israel, it will be over for the United States. God will remove His presence from us and leave us to face the consequences of our sin.

It would seem that we'd have a heart to serve God because He's forgiven us of our sins and we're going to be taken up to heaven, but we don't. In our minds, we are afraid that if we serve God, we're going to suffer. Satan has us convinced that if we surrender something to God, He's going to take it away. And in truth, sometimes He does. However, we need to know that if God takes something away, He's going to give it back to us a hundred-fold. God always lifts up human beings; He does not tear them down, whereas Satan's goal is to bring us down and destroy our life.

Sin and Satan will also seek to blind us from the work of God in our life; they seek to keep us away from the things of the Spirit. We become deaf to the call of God when we're doing things that we ought not to be doing. Sometimes we are blinded from seeing the need of the people around us because we're too focused on ourselves. The Bible says we are to be praying for and helping other people. When we're self-centered, we're blinded. When we only want to take care of our own needs, we are unaware of the needs around us. Sin will always blind us and bring us down. Satan is seeking to tie us down, to bring us into bondage, and to bring us under his authority and power. What is the answer? We need to turn to Christ and run to the cross. When we realize we are sinning, we need to repent immediately. Victory will always come when we turn to the cross.

God Rebukes Samson

"Now the lords of the Philistines gathered together to offer a great sacrifice to Dagon their god, and to rejoice. And they said: 'Our god has delivered into our hands Samson our enemy!' When the people saw him, they praised their god; for they said: 'Our god has delivered into our hands our enemy, the destroyer of our land, and the one who multiplied our dead' " (Judges 16:23–24).

Samson spent his whole life running from God, and it caused him to lose everything. God first had to rebuke Samson before He could restore him. The Lord rebuked Samson because his testimony brought shame to the name of God. It's important that we do not violate our testimony. If we go out and sin, we're going to shame the name of Jesus Christ; we're going to hurt our marriage and our ministry; and we're going to hurt other believers. There's just too much at stake when it comes to God's name. He saved us and was willing to put His life into ours; we need to honor His testimony in us for the rest of our life.

Samson's testimony was ruined. The Philistines were saying, "Our god has destroyed Jehovah," and in their minds, they were right. Their god Dagon had the victory—he had destroyed the man of God. The world rejoices when Christians fall. The crazy thing about sin is that it will lure us, love us, please us, and play with us; then it will turn on us, mock us, and finally shame us in front of the world. Samson's life was an embarrassment. He was always entertaining the enemy. Once a revered judge, he became the butt of jokes. Once a man of God, he then became a celebrity in the enemy camp. Once a mighty man of God, he became blind, old, bald, and weak. But God was not yet finished with Samson.

God's Ability to Restore

We have a merciful God. When we blow it, God is willing to give us a second chance—to restore us. It is the mercy and grace of God that give us not only a second chance, but multiple chances. And God loves to turn the tables on the enemy. In the book of Esther, Haman (who worked for the king) was seeking to kill the Jews. Mordecai (Esther's uncle and guardian) went to Queen Esther and said, "Listen, you need to go before the king and tell him what is happening." She answered, "I can't do that because he's kind of in a bad mood, and he doesn't want to be bothered. If I interrupt the king, I could die unless he tips the scepter toward me." (Even though Esther was married to the king, she feared him.)

Then Mordecai said, "Listen, how do you know if you have not come to the palace for such a time as this?" With God's conviction upon her, Esther walked through the door to the king, saying, "If I perish, I perish." As it happened, the king lovingly tipped the scepter toward her, and she was then able to share with him about Haman's intention to kill the Jews. When the king was able to see what was taking place, he put a stop to it. In the end, Haman lost his life on the very gallows that he had built to kill Mordecai and the Jews. God loves to turn the tables.

We need to understand that in our life, God will turn the tables for us too. God can cause the "kings" in our life to tip their scepter toward us as well and set circumstances right. God can and will vindicate our life. It might not happen overnight or even within our timetable, but God will do the work in a very powerful way—His way.

God Restores Samson

Samson turned back to God, and the Lord restored him. God desires to take our wasted lives and make them trophies of His grace. Although we fall into sin, God will instantly forgive us if we ask Him. But there are some things that take time, just as it took time for Samson's hair to grow back. Restoration doesn't come quickly. We need to have patience, because it is in the process of restoration that we grow and change. But we want it now! I know, but it's better we wait for God's time and plan to accomplish it right than to enact our own destruction. The story in the book of Joshua, chapter 6, when God's people took the city of Jericho, is an example of them following God's way; because of that, the walls of Jericho came down. But when God's people went to the city of Ai in chapter 7, they did not consult the Lord before they attacked and, consequently, lost the battle. Only after obeying the Lord's command did they prevail over Ai.

This is a great lesson for us to learn: God's ways are much easier than our ways, and when we refuse to do things His way, it's much harder to gain any ground at all. Jericho came down quickly because God's people were in His perfect will. Ai defeated Israel because the Israelites were out of God's will. Yet when God's people repented and did it His way, they received the victory at Ai. So, yes, we are able to conquer territory that we initially lost, but it's always harder. God does want us to have that territory, but it's going to take longer to get it due to our own blundering in trying to

> *God's ways are much easier than our ways, and when we refuse to do things His way, it's much harder to gain any ground at all.*

achieve it in our own way and in our own timing. And in truth, we may never receive it in exactly the way that God had originally intended for us; our sin may have colored it. Remember that God forgave David for his sin against Bathsheba and Uriah, but David could never again do whatever he wanted to do. He desired to build the temple for God, but God said, "No, you're a bloody man." The apostle Peter was restored and forgiven, and God did a great work in his life, but the apostle Paul was right on his tail ready to take over his ministry. Jonah was restored after running away from God and being spit up on the beach by a whale, but he faded from the scene and was never heard from again. And Elijah was restored after he wanted to commit suicide, but Elisha took over his ministry.

It's important to keep in mind that although God will graciously restore us, it may not be to the heights we once were. Are we a Samson who dove too deep, for too long, into a life of sin, only to be fully restored to what we once could have been? Are we a David, a Peter, or a Jonah? If we don't want to be any of these men, if instead we want to rise to the greatest height of God's will for us, we must continually evaluate our life and ask the Lord to remove every vestige of sin that may have crept in.

God Reuses Samson

God restored Samson and used him one final time before he died. In Judges 16:28–30, Samson asked the Lord to remember him, to strengthen him, and to let him die. Samson's first request was for the Lord to remember him because he wanted God to once again look upon him with favor. Maybe we are in financial trouble or just lost our job. If we're able to say, "Lord, remember me," it means we're a man or woman of faith. When we ask the Lord to remember us, it is a way of surrendering our will to His. In other words, we are seeking the Lord's favor upon our life in the midst of the situation in which we find ourselves.

Samson's second request of the Lord was to give him strength just once more. After all this time, Samson finally acknowledged God as the source of his strength. Even so, I don't believe the Lord answered Samson's prayer for the reason it was asked. Samson wanted his strength back so he could avenge himself. Remember, the Philistines had blinded him—but God didn't want to avenge the loss of his eyes. God doesn't want us to take revenge on people who have hurt us; He wants us to learn from it.

And finally, the moment we acknowledge that it is God who is our strength and our avenger and we cry out, "God, let me die," that is the time He does the work. God gave Samson his strength back not to avenge himself, but to restore his purpose and his mission. When Samson asked God to let him die, the Lord then used him as an instrument to wipe out the enemy. That is why Samson was made a judge in the first place: to bring Israel back to God and to destroy the enemy—the Philistines.

The life of Samson, God's servant, began as a miracle. He grew up with godly parents, and the Lord blessed him. He was also given great strength. But Samson's life changed after he began disobeying God. Eventually, the enemy shaved his head, blinded him, beat him, and put him in prison. By all outward appearances, they had defeated him. Although once an unbeatably strong man, Samson was broken as he entered into his final moments of life.

The Philistines were gathered in the temple of their god when they called for Samson to come and perform for them. At that critical moment, Samson knew he was standing before a multitude of people. Although he was not able to see, his ears were wide open to the noise and laughter of the crowd. The scene is described in Judges 16:27: *"Now the temple was full of men and women. All the lords of the Philistines were there—about three thousand men and women on the roof watching while Samson performed."* Basically, the Philistines wanted to make fun of and laugh at this blind, tortured, and once arrogant man.

Humbled, Samson had to ask a child to lead him to the pillars. After many years of rebelling, a broken Samson turned back to God in the final moments of his life and cried out: "Lord, remember me. Lord, strengthen me. Lord, let me bow before you. Lord, let me once again give you all my might." And Samson's final words were, *"Let me die with the Philistines!"* (Judges 16:30). At that moment, he bowed himself with all his strength, and God honored his requests and used him mightily to destroy many Philistines. Samson repented, God's presence returned, Samson pushed the pillars with all of his might, and the temple fell, killing all the Philistines present.

God Will Take a Failure and Make a Trophy of Grace

The story of Samson is a story about God's grace. The Lord is able to take a failure and turn it into a trophy of His grace. Maybe we've been living for years as a failure. Maybe we've been a failure as a father, as a spouse, as a leader in the community, as an employee—it doesn't make a difference. God makes a difference! God is extending His heart to us and saying, "I have been restoring failures from the beginning. I'm in the restoration business, and there's no one better at it than Me. However, there's a right way and a wrong way to live. If you come My way and bow, I will change your life for the better." God is asking us, "Will you trust Me? Will you give Me your life? Are you willing to die to yourself?" Selfishness will destroy our life, but the moment we are willing to die to ourselves and turn to Him, God has something special for us. God will restore us and reuse us. It's never too late for God to work in our lives for His glory.

God's favor was upon Samson. The successes he enjoyed were purely from God because the Lord moved in and through him. God blessed his life when he least deserved it. That's called *amazing grace*. In fact, the Holy Spirit came upon Samson during the worst moments of his life, to save his life and to keep him in God's calling even when he was clearly out of control and unable to do so himself.

God's grace is not only amazing, but it is also absolutely life-changing. If we find ourselves going down a particular road, having a horrible time, and completely falling apart, we should not be surprised when God suddenly redeems us with the power of the Holy Spirit, rescuing us and restoring us unto Himself. Because God has a purpose for our life, He is not going to give up on us. Even in the midst of Samson's horrible disobedience, God used him. The Spirit of God is able to take even our mistakes and use them for His glory. Remember that God is always able to redeem us regardless of the sin or circumstance in which we find ourselves entangled. There is no need to go any further in a sinful situation or in our stubbornness. However, it is a matter of choice. It is our choice how we live our lives.

> *God has a purpose for our life, He is not going to give up on us.*

Final Moments

Samson's redemption did not occur until the very end of his life. Those final moments of his life are more significant than all the other moments combined simply because at that point, he finally submitted to God's will for his life. It wasn't until Samson finally prayed an honest prayer and called out to God with all of his heart that he began to live for God. The moment Samson cried out, God honored him in spite of all he had done in the past. The Lord, in His tender mercy, wrote this belated servant—Samson—into the Hall of Faith. The author of the book of Hebrews wrote, *"And what more shall I say? For the time would fail me to tell of Gideon and Barak and Samson and Jephthah, also of David and Samuel and the prophets: who through faith subdued kingdoms, worked righteousness, obtained promises, stopped the mouths of lions, quenched the violence of fire, escaped the edge of the sword, out of weakness were made strong, became valiant in battle, turned to flight the armies of the aliens"* (Hebrews 11:32–34).

Reading in the New Testament that Samson was listed in the Hall of Faith causes me to rejoice because then I know there is hope for me. We need to quit trying to live life on our own terms and start trusting God. We need to recognize our weaknesses and start looking to His supernatural power. We need to stay faithful to His call and let all other lovers go. If Samson could, so can we. Samson's place in the Hall of Faith is no mistake. He was chosen, called, and gifted by God to accomplish His purpose. God has our place reserved in the Hall of Faith as well.

God answered Samson's final prayer. When we bow our hearts before the Lord, He will answer our prayer as well. When we can say, "God, I'm willing to die to myself," God will always answer that prayer and do a work in our life. Through all Samson's rebellion, arrogance, selfishness, and pride, God continued to uphold Samson, even to the very end. Samson's life may have been a wasted one, but in God's eyes, it was never worthless. In his final moments, he humbled himself and submitted to God's authority. He allowed God to change him; that is why he is included in the Hall of Faith. We don't have to live a wasted life. Living for ourselves, fulfilling our own desires, and doing things our way will cause us to miss out on the abundance of God's blessings. Yet just as Samson humbled himself in the last few minutes of his life, so can we—in an instant—humble ourselves before the Lord and live our life as God intended.

Let us die to our pride and to our selfishness. Let us die to our flesh! I want to be a trophy of God's amazing grace, and I know you do too. It's never too late. I invite you today to humble yourself, turn to Christ, and run to the cross.

Final Points to Ponder:

- Am I quick to repent, or do I give Satan a foothold in my life?

- Who is on the throne of my heart? My flesh and the Spirit of God cannot both have dominion. My flesh must die.

- Do I realize that it is never too late to humbly turn to God?

Jesus, Lover of my soul
Jesus, I will never let You go,
You've taken me from the miry clay,
You've set my feet upon the Rock, and now I know,
I love You, I need You,
Though my world may fall, I'll never let You go.

Written by
John Ezzy, Daniel Grul, and Stephen McPherson
Published by
Hillsong Publishing

For more information, contact:
Calvary Chapel South Bay
19300 S. Vermont Avenue
Gardena, California 90248
(310) 352-3333
Websites:
www.ccsouthbay.org
www.lightoftheword.org

OTHER MATERIALS AVAILABLE BY STEVE MAYS

CHOICES
Who Will You Serve?

Life is full of choices. Have you ever made a bad choice? Was the outcome filled with pain, despondency, or a feeling of failure? Choices are your responsibility, but the choices made today will determine the outcome of your future.

Using the Old Testament book of Joshua as his text, Pastor Steve Mays takes an in-depth look at the choices that knock at the door of your life daily and the impact those choices have in life. Furthermore, Steve will give practical counsel to challenge and encourage you to make good and effective decisions. Immediately you will discover how good decisions will bring deeper dedication to the Lord, which will result in greater joy and peace.

A TOUCH OF LIGHT POCKET BOOKLETS

These tiny inspirational topical booklets contain perfect little nuggets of information for everyday living. Each booklet addresses specific areas of our lives that will help with our daily walk with the Lord. "Our Only Hope is God" reminds us that in the midst of a crisis, we need to turn to God. "When God Begins to Knock" asks the question, What happens when God begins asking you questions? It's a Father reaching out—helping us to build our life and faith. "Let Go & Let God" teaches us to learn the freedom and encouragement that comes when we look to God and cast our cares upon Him.

A LIFE OUT OF CONTROL

Steve Mays takes a look at the problem of lust (not just physical, but also the type of lust that makes us want what we want and ignore God's will) and how our lives can so easily spin out of control. By taking a look at the life of Samson, Pastor Steve helps us see the danger of rebellion and how to find freedom through Jesus Christ.

A SMOLDERING FIRE

Try as hard as we might to obey the Ten Commandments, we fail—time and time again. Steve Mays takes a look at the problem of sin and how it can lie dormant for years but never die. Though we can never be "sinless" in our fleshly body, we can have victory over habitual sin by heeding the warning signs; fleeing from temptation; and relying on the Holy Spirit's power and presence to guide us into righteousness.

THE FAITHFUL FAMILY

If you have a family, you are certainly aware of the attacks from the enemy to tear your family apart. But how do you combat these attacks? How do you deal with circumstances that seem out of your control? Steve Mays provides some practical advice starting with a goal to build and maintain a healthy, loving family. It's built on a foundation that is devoted to Jesus Christ and centered on prayer.

THE WORLD'S SMALLEST TROUBLEMAKER

The words that come from our mouths–do they build up or tear down? Do they encourage or discourage others? How we use our tongue affects the lives of others. Do the things you say reflect the goodness of God or the evil of Satan? In this insightful bookle, we learn practical ways to tame the world's smallest troublemaker. May the words of our mouths and the meditation of our hearts be acceptable in the sight of our LORD.

A HEARTBEAT FROM HELL
...a choice for life

Steve Mays was desperate, hopeless, and sleeping in gutters. He was living with a group of guys who were involved in motorcycle gangs. A .38-caliber bullet had penetrated his left leg; the authorities wanted Steve for questioning. Then one day something happened—Steve became a new man. His whole life changed. This booklet was birthed from the life story of a man who at one point was a heartbeat from hell but by God's grace made a choice for life. He's been there, and he's done that. At the end of it all, he found himself in the arms of a God who loves him, and forgives him. For over 30 years, Steve Mays is the senior pastor of Calvary Chapel South Bay, which has an attendance of over 9,000 weekly, in Gardena, California. He has a national radio broadcast, "Light of the Word," which is heard on many radio stations throughout the country. He is a graduate of Azusa Pacific University with a master's degree in Theology and was also awarded an honorary Doctor of Divinity Degree at APU.

We encourage you to visit Calvary Chapel South Bay's website at www.ccsouthbay.org if you want to order additional copies of *Crossing the Line* or Steve Mays' other books, *Heartbeat from Hell (English or Spanish versions)*, *Choices* or any of his other booklets or pamphlets. Additional information and audio messages by Steve Mays are also available online or you may contact us by calling 310-352-3333 or by writing to:

Calvary Chapel South Bay
19300 S. Vermont Avenue
Gardena, CA 90248